Google Certified Professional Cloud Architect Exam Prep

450 Practice Questions

1st Edition

www.versatileread.com

Document Control

Proposal Name	:	Google Certified Professional Cloud Architect Exam Prep: 450 Practice Questions
Document Edition	:	1st
Document Release Date	:	29th June 2024
Reference	:	PCA
VR Product Code	:	20242302PCA

Feedback:

If you have any comments regarding the quality of this book or otherwise alter it to better suit your needs, you can contact us through email at info@versatileread.com

Please make sure to include the book's title and ISBN in your message.

VERSAtile Reads

About the Contributors:

Nouman Ahmed Khan

AWS/Azure/GCP-Architect, CCDE, CCIEx5 (R&S, SP, Security, DC, Wireless), CISSP, CISA, CISM, CRISC, ISO27K-LA is a Solution Architect working with a global telecommunication provider. He works with enterprises, mega-projects, and service providers to help them select the best-fit technology solutions. He also works as a consultant to understand customer business processes and helps select an appropriate technology strategy to support business goals. He has more than eighteen years of experience working with global clients. One of his notable experiences was his tenure with a large managed security services provider, where he was responsible for managing the complete MSSP product portfolio. With his extensive knowledge and expertise in various areas of technology, including cloud computing, network infrastructure, security, and risk management, Nouman has become a trusted advisor for his clients.

Abubakar Saeed

Abubakar Saeed is a trailblazer in the realm of technology and innovation. With a rich professional journey spanning over twenty-nine years, Abubakar has seamlessly blended his expertise in engineering with his passion for transformative leadership. Starting humbly at the grassroots level, he has significantly contributed to pioneering the Internet in Pakistan and beyond. Abubakar's multifaceted experience encompasses managing, consulting, designing, and implementing projects, showcasing his versatility as a leader.

His exceptional skills shine in leading businesses, where he champions innovation and transformation. Abubakar stands as a testament to the power of visionary leadership, heading operations, solutions design, and integration. His emphasis on adhering to project timelines and exceeding customer expectations has set him apart as a great leader. With an unwavering commitment to adopting technology for operational simplicity and enhanced efficiency, Abubakar Saeed continues to inspire and drive change in the industry.

Dr. Fahad Abdali

Dr. Fahad Abdali is an esteemed leader with an outstanding twenty-year track record in managing diverse businesses. With a stellar educational background, including a bachelor's degree from the prestigious NED University of Engineers & Technology and a Ph.D. from the University of Karachi, Dr. Abdali epitomizes academic excellence and continuous professional growth.

Dr. Abdali's leadership journey is marked by his unwavering commitment to innovation and his astute understanding of industry dynamics. His ability to navigate intricate challenges has driven growth and nurtured organizational triumph. Driven by a passion for excellence, he stands as a beacon of inspiration within the business realm. With his remarkable leadership skills, Dr. Fahad Abdali continues to steer businesses toward unprecedented success, making him a true embodiment of a great leader.

Muniza Kamran

Muniza Kamran is a technical content developer in a professional field. She crafts clear and informative content that simplifies complex technical concepts for diverse audiences, with a passion for technology. Her expertise lies in Microsoft, cybersecurity, cloud security and emerging technologies, making her a valuable asset in the tech industry. Her dedication to quality and accuracy ensures that her writing empowers readers with valuable insights and knowledge. She has done certification in SQL database, database design, cloud solution architecture, and NDG Linux unhatched from CISCO.

Table of Contents

About Certified Professional Cloud Architect (PCA) Exam

Introduction

Introducing the Google Cloud Professional Cloud Architect (PCA) certification validates an individual's expertise in designing, developing, and managing secure, scalable, and robust solutions on the Google Cloud Platform (GCP). This certification encompasses responsibilities such as designing cloud solution architectures, managing cloud infrastructure, ensuring security and compliance, optimizing technical processes, and maintaining solution reliability. Achieving the Google Certified PCA certification offers significant career benefits, including enhanced job opportunities, increased earning potential, and validation of your skills. The exam covers key areas like solution design, infrastructure management, security, and compliance, requiring a strategic approach to preparation, hands-on experience, and a thorough understanding of GCP services.

What is Google Certified Professional Cloud Architecture?

A Google Cloud Professional Cloud Architect is a certification offered by Google Cloud Platform (GCP) that validates an individual's expertise in designing, developing, and managing robust, secure, scalable, highly available, and dynamic solutions to drive business objectives. The responsibilities of a Professional Cloud Architect include designing and planning cloud solution architectures, managing and provisioning cloud infrastructure, ensuring security and compliance, optimizing technical and business processes, managing the implementation of cloud architectures, and ensuring solution reliability. Key competencies involve a deep understanding of cloud architecture and GCP, security and compliance, infrastructure management, solution development, cloud migration, and cost optimization.

Why should you take Google Certified PCA?

Obtaining the Google Cloud Professional Cloud Architect certification offers several advantages:

- **In-Demand Profession:** The rapid evolution of cloud computing has created a high demand for cloud architecture experts. As a Google Cloud Certified Professional Cloud Architect, you position yourself as a sought-after professional in this dynamic field.
- **Lucrative Compensation:** Google Cloud-certified cloud architects often command competitive salaries due to the strong demand for their skills. Specialized knowledge in cloud architecture can lead to attractive remuneration packages.
- **Versatile Expertise:** Cloud architects bridge the gap between business and technology with in-depth knowledge of cloud platforms, infrastructure, security, and scalability. This role allows you to develop a versatile skill set, opening doors to diverse career opportunities within cloud computing.
- **Impactful Role:** As a cloud architect, you play a pivotal role in designing, implementing, and managing cloud-based solutions for organizations. Your work can shape technological infrastructures, optimize operations, and contribute to business growth and success.
- **Continuous Learning:** Cloud computing continually evolves, requiring professionals to stay abreast of the latest technologies and best practices. Working as a Google Cloud Certified Professional Cloud Architect exposes you to ongoing learning opportunities,

enabling you to expand your knowledge and skills as the field advances.

- **Google Cloud Platform (GCP) Excellence**: With Google Cloud being a leading service provider, expertise in GCP provides a competitive edge. The Google Cloud Certified Professional Cloud Architect certification showcases your proficiency in designing and implementing cloud solutions on GCP, a highly valued skill for organizations utilizing or considering adopting the Google Cloud Platform.

Prerequisites for the Google Certified PCA Exam

The Google Certified Professional Cloud Architect (PCA) exam does not have strict prerequisites in terms of required experience or previous certifications. However, candidates should have a basic understanding of cloud architecture principles and familiarity with Google Cloud Platform (GCP) services.

The intended audience for the Google Certified PCA Certification Course?

The intended audience for the Google Cloud Professional Cloud Architect (PCA) certification course includes:

- **Cloud Architects**: Individuals who are responsible for designing, developing, and managing cloud solutions on Google Cloud Platform (GCP). This certification validates their expertise in cloud architecture and their ability to design scalable, secure, and highly available cloud solutions to meet business requirements.
- **Cloud Engineers:** Professionals involved in implementing and maintaining cloud infrastructure on GCP. The certification helps them deepen their understanding of cloud architecture principles and best practices, enabling them to contribute effectively to the design and deployment of cloud solutions.
- **Solution Architects:** Those tasked with designing and implementing solutions to solve business challenges using cloud

technologies. The certification equips them with the knowledge and skills necessary to design and optimize cloud architectures on GCP, ensuring alignment with organizational goals and requirements.

- **System Administrators:** Individuals responsible for managing and maintaining cloud environments on GCP. The certification provides them with a comprehensive understanding of GCP services and their interdependencies, enabling them to design and manage scalable and reliable cloud infrastructure.

- **IT Professionals**: Professionals working in various IT roles who wish to transition to cloud computing or enhance their skills in cloud architecture. The certification serves as a valuable credential that demonstrates their proficiency in designing and implementing cloud solutions on GCP.

The Certification Exam

The Google Cloud Professional Cloud Architect (PCA) exam evaluates candidates' understanding of several key areas. Specifically, it assesses their ability to design, develop, and manage robust, secure, scalable, highly available, and dynamic solutions to drive business objectives. Here are the main domains the exam focuses on:

1. **Designing and Planning a Cloud Solution Architecture:**
   - Designing a solution infrastructure that meets business and technical requirements.
   - Planning and designing network architecture.
   - Designing a migration plan.
   - Ensuring solution and operations reliability.

2. **Managing and Provisioning a Solution Infrastructure:**
   - Configuring network topologies.
   - Configuring compute systems and storage systems.
   - Implementing security and ensuring compliance.
   - Managing identity and access management.

3. **Designing for Security and Compliance:**

- Designing for security.
- Designing for compliance.
- Analyzing and defining technical processes.
- Ensuring the implementation meets the business and compliance requirements.

4. **Analyzing and Optimizing Technical and Business Processes:**
   - Analyzing and defining technical and business processes.
   - Recommending options to optimize business processes.
   - Managing implementation to meet business requirements.

5. **Managing Implementations of Cloud Architecture:**
   - Managing solution and infrastructure life cycle.
   - Ensuring the implementation meets reliability requirements.
   - Ensuring operational efficiency.

6. **Ensuring Solution and Operations Reliability:**
   - Designing for business and technical requirements.
   - Designing for security and compliance.
   - Designing for operations.
   - Managing solution operations to ensure performance.

7. **Case Study Analysis:**
   - Applying knowledge of GCP products and services to case studies.
   - Designing and managing a solution to meet specific requirements provided in case studies.
   - Making implementation recommendations based on given constraints.

Exam Preparation

Before Exam

To prepare for the Google Cloud Professional Cloud Architect (PCA) certification exam, start by reviewing the exam guide provided by Google Cloud Platform (GCP). Then, use various resources like whitepapers, official documentation, online courses, and practice exams to reinforce your understanding of key concepts. Hands-on experience and regular self-assessment are crucial for success. Stay updated on exam changes and adjust your study plan accordingly.

Day of Exam

Preparing for the Google Cloud Professional Cloud Architect (PCA) exam demands thorough preparation and focus. On exam day, ensure to arrive early at the testing center for smooth check-in procedures. Bring all required documents, including valid identification and any materials specified by the exam center.

During the exam, maintain a composed and focused mindset. Manage any nervousness by taking deep breaths and carefully reading each question to understand its requirements fully. Stay confident in your abilities and manage your time effectively. If faced with challenging questions, consider flagging them for later review if time permits.

After Exam

After finishing the Google Cloud Professional Cloud Architect (PCA) exam, it's crucial to assess your performance. Identify your strengths and areas needing improvement. If allowed, review missed questions to understand why you answered them incorrectly and learn from those mistakes. This reflective process enhances your understanding and prepares you better for future exams or real-world applications.

Exam Information

Prior Certification		Exam Validity	
Not Required		2 Years	
Exam Fee		Exam Duration	
$200 USD		120 Minutes	
No. of Questions		Passing Marks	
50(Approx.)		80% (Approx.)	
Recommended Experience			
3+ years of industry experience- 1+ years of designing & managing solutions on Google Cloud			
Exam Format			
Multiple Choice/ Multiple Select			

Google Certified PCA Exam Preparation Pointers

Preparing for the Google Cloud Professional Cloud Architect (PCA) exam requires a strategic approach. Here are some pointers to guide your preparation:

1. **Understand the Exam Guide:** Start by thoroughly reviewing the exam guide provided by Google Cloud Platform (GCP). Familiarize yourself with the domains, topics, and weighting of each section.
2. **Study Resources:** Utilize a variety of resources such as GCP whitepapers, official documentation, online courses, and practice exams. Ensure you cover key architectural principles, design patterns, and best practices for building solutions on Google Cloud Platform.
3. **Hands-on Experience**: Gain practical experience by working with GCP services. Take advantage of labs, projects, and real-world scenarios to reinforce your understanding and skills.

4. **Practice Exams:** Regularly assess your knowledge with practice exams and quizzes. Identify areas where you need additional review and focus your efforts accordingly.

5. **Time Management:** Practice time management during your preparation and the exam itself. Allocate sufficient time to each section and question, and learn to pace yourself effectively.

6. **Stay Updated:** Keep abreast of any updates or changes to the exam blueprint. Adjust your study plan accordingly to ensure you're covering the latest topics and requirements.

7. **Review and Reflect:** After completing practice exams or the actual exam, assess your performance. Identify strengths and areas for improvement and review missed questions to understand the underlying concepts better.

Job Opportunities with Google Certified PCA Certifications

The Google Certified Professional Cloud Architect (PCA) certification validates your expertise in designing, developing, and managing secure, scalable, and cost-effective solutions on the Google Cloud Platform (GCP). While it demonstrates a high level of knowledge, there are various job opportunities you can pursue with a Google Certified PCA certification:

Cloud Architect Roles:

- **GCP Solutions Architect:** Collaborate with stakeholders to design and implement complex cloud solutions on GCP, ensuring they meet business needs and technical requirements.
- **Enterprise Architect (Cloud Focus):** Lead the design and implementation of cloud architecture for large organizations, leveraging GCP as a primary platform.
- **Cloud Migration Architect:** Plan and execute cloud migration strategies for applications and infrastructure to GCP, ensuring a smooth and successful transition.

Cloud Engineering Roles:

- **Senior Cloud Engineer:** Design, develop, and maintain complex cloud infrastructure and applications on GCP, focusing on scalability, security, and performance.
- **Site Reliability Engineer (SRE) - GCP Focus:** Automate operations, monitor system health, and ensure high availability and reliability of cloud-based solutions on GCP.
- **DevOps Engineer (GCP Specialization):** Bridge the gap between development and operations, utilizing GCP tools and services for continuous integration and deployment (CI/CD) pipelines.

Other Potential Opportunities:

- **Cloud Security Architect:** Design and implement secure cloud architecture on GCP, adhering to best practices and compliance regulations.
- **Cloud Data Architect:** Design and manage data solutions on GCP, including data storage, processing, and analytics.
- **Cloud Cost Optimization Specialist:** Analyze and optimize cloud resource utilization on GCP to ensure cost-effectiveness and avoid unnecessary spending.

Demand for Google Certified PCA Certification in 2024

The demand for the Google Certified Professional Cloud Architect (PCA) certification is expected to remain strong in 2024, driven by several factors:

- **Surging Cloud Adoption:** Cloud computing continues its explosive growth across industries. Businesses are increasingly seeking skilled professionals to design, develop, and manage their cloud infrastructure. The Google Certified PCA validates expertise in these critical areas, making it highly valuable.
- **Highly Specialized Skill:** The Google Certified PCA signifies a high level of knowledge and practical experience in GCP architecture. This advanced skillset is in short supply as companies prioritize building robust and secure cloud solutions on GCP.

- **Evolving Cloud Landscape:** Cloud platforms like GCP are constantly evolving, introducing new features and functionalities. The Google Certified PCA demonstrates a commitment to keeping pace with these advancements, ensuring your knowledge remains relevant.

Practice Questions

1. Which of the following is a primary consideration when starting the planning phase for a cloud solution?
A. Technical details about the current solution
B. Business requirements
C. Network architecture
D. High availability configuration

2. What is a key benefit of using managed services in cloud architecture?
A. Increased capital expenditure
B. Reduced workload on systems administrators and DevOps engineers
C. Longer deployment times
D. Increased manual intervention in processes

3. Which type of virtual machines are cost-effective for tasks that can be easily recovered and restarted?
A. On-demand VMs
B. Reserved VMs
C. Preemptible VMs
D. Dedicated VMs

4. How does autoscaling help in reducing operational expenses?
A. By maintaining a fixed number of instances
B. By increasing the number of instances during low-demand
C. By adjusting the number of instances to meet the immediate need
D. By requiring manual intervention to scale instances

5. What is a common trait of business requirements in cloud architecture?
A. They can be satisfied by a single technical decision
B. They are always about reducing operational expenses

C. They are rarely satisfied by a single technical decision

D. They do not impact customer experience

6. Which practice supports rapid development, testing, deployment, and feedback in software development?

A. Waterfall development

B. Agile software development

C. Monolithic application development

D. Manual code integration

7. What is the main advantage of continuous integration and continuous deployment (CI/CD)?

A. Releasing large amounts of new code at one time

B. Integrating small amounts of new code frequently

C. Increased manual debugging

D. Delayed feedback from colleagues and customers

8. When might a business consider a lift-and-shift migration approach?

A. When the application requires substantial modification to run in the cloud

B. To avoid a large capital expenditure on new equipment

C. When decomposing the application into microservices

D. When rewriting the application is necessary

9. Which factor should be assessed to decide if a monolithic application can be migrated to the cloud with minimal modification?

A. The application's dependency on deprecated components

B. The language in which the application is written

C. The application's current performance

D. The number of users accessing the application

10. Which department might only need access to their systems during business hours, allowing for maintenance during off-hours?
A. Sales department
B. Customer support department
C. Finance department
D. Logistics department

11. Which of the following best describes a Service-Level Objective (SLO)?
A. A budget for capital expenditures
B. An agreement between a service provider and a customer
C. A measure of performance against specific objectives
D. An expense from the operating budget

12. What is the purpose of Cloud Operations logging in the context of service-level objectives?
A. To increase capital expenditures
B. To create a budget for operational costs
C. To collect information about significant events
D. To manage personnel data

13. What is the main focus of the Health Insurance Portability and Accountability Act (HIPAA)?
A. Financial reporting
B. Data protection for credit card processing
C. Privacy of healthcare information
D. Online privacy for children

14. Which of the following is an example of an operational expenditure (Opex)?
A. Purchasing new computer equipment
B. Buying land for a new office

C. Allocating funds for daily business operations

D. Investing in long-term assets

15. What is a Key Performance Indicator (KPI)?

A. A regulation for protecting customer data

B. A measure of performance for achieving key objectives

C. A procedure to ensure policy compliance

D. A type of capital expenditure

16. How can reducing the time to recover from an incident be achieved?

A. By increasing capital expenditures

B. By collecting metrics and log events for quick access during incidents

C. By focusing only on operational expenditures

D. By ignoring small incidents

17. What type of regulation is the Sarbanes-Oxley Act (SOX)?

A. A healthcare regulation

B. A financial reporting regulation

C. A privacy regulation

D. A data protection regulation for credit card processing

18. What is the primary objective of digital transformation in businesses?

A. To reduce the number of employees

B. To decrease operational expenditures

C. To adopt information technologies for major business improvements

D. To increase capital expenditures

19. Which of the following is a characteristic of a brick-and-mortar business?

A. It has a significant online presence

B. It operates primarily in the digital space

C. It has a physical presence, such as retail stores

D. It only engages in online transactions

20. What does the term 'governance' refer to in an organizational context?

A. The allocation of funds for daily operations

B. The acquisition of long-term assets

C. The procedures and practices to ensure policy compliance

D. The regulations for protecting customer data

21. Which of the following services is the best choice for running a virtual machine with a specific hardened version of Linux?

A. App Engine Flexible

B. Kubernetes Engine

C. Compute Engine

D. Cloud Functions

22. If you need a globally consistent transactional data store for your application, which Google Cloud service should you choose?

A. Cloud SQL

B. BigQuery

C. Spanner

D. Cloud Datastore

23. Which of the following storage classes in Cloud Storage is designed for data that will be accessed no more than once a year?

A. Regional

B. Multiregional

C. Coldline

D. Nearline

24. What networking option should you choose if you need a bandwidth requirement of 10 Gbps or greater for connecting an on-premises data center to the Google Cloud Platform?
A. Virtual Private Network (VPN)
B. Partner Interconnect
C. Dedicated Interconnect
D. VPC Peering

25. Which service would be the best option for a document store requiring a flexible schema?
A. BigQuery
B. Cloud Datastore
C. Cloud SQL
D. Spanner

26. Which of the following metrics is an example of a Service-Level Indicator (SLI)?
A. Availability of 99.99%
B. Latency
C. Durability
D. Scalability

27. Which Google Cloud service should you use to ingest large volumes of time-series data at low latency?
A. BigQuery
B. Cloud Datastore
C. Cloud SQL
D. Bigtable

28. What is a key benefit of using autoscalers and instance groups in Compute Engine for scalability?

A. Reduced data redundancy

B. Automated encryption

C. Managed backups

D. Adapting infrastructure to load

29. If you need a regional-scale relational database and prefer a managed service, which Google Cloud offering should you choose?

A. Spanner

B. Cloud SQL

C. BigQuery

D. Cloud Datastore

30. Which networking component is essential for structuring virtual private clouds (VPCs) and managing traffic rules?

A. Cloud CDN

B. Firewalls and firewall rules

C. Cloud Load Balancing

D. Cloud VPN

31. What is the primary reason Dress4Win is committing to a full migration to a public cloud?

A. To reduce advertising costs

B. To mitigate the limitations of their current infrastructure

C. To eliminate the need for a disaster recovery site

D. To stop using Ubuntu

32. Which component is NOT part of Dress4Win's existing technical environment?

A. MySQL databases

B. Redis servers

C. Microsoft SQL Server databases

D. Apache Hadoop/Spark servers

33. What is a key business requirement for Dress4Win's cloud migration?

A. Reduce the number of development environments

B. Improve business agility and speed of innovation

C. Eliminate the need for Redis servers

D. Migrate only the production environment

34. Which technical requirement is essential for Dress4Win's cloud strategy?

A. Implement a multi-cloud environment

B. Support failover of the production environment to the cloud during an emergency

C. Use only one private connection between the production data center and cloud environment

D. Avoid encrypting data on the wire

35. What is the main concern of Dress4Win's investors regarding the current infrastructure?

A. High advertising costs

B. Inability to scale and contain costs

C. Low traffic during weekends

D. Overuse of Redis servers

36. Which of the following statements describes an opportunity for using autoscaling at Dress4Win?

A. Traffic patterns are consistent throughout the day.

B. Traffic patterns are highest in the mornings and weekend evenings.

C. All servers run Windows.

D. Redis servers are always fully utilized.

37. Which storage appliance is used for logs and backups at Dress4Win?
A. iSCSI
B. Fiber channel SAN
C. NAS
D. Local disks

38. What kind of servers does Dress4Win use for data analysis and real-time trending calculations?
A. Web application servers
B. RabbitMQ servers
C. Apache Hadoop/Spark servers
D. Miscellaneous servers

39. Which component in Dress4Win's technical environment handles social notifications and events?
A. Redis servers
B. RabbitMQ servers
C. MySQL databases
D. Jenkins servers

40. What is a business requirement related to security for Dress4Win's cloud migration?
A. Implement a multi-cloud strategy
B. Improve security by defining and adhering to a set of security and IAM best practices
C. Avoid using encryption
D. Support only public connections between the data center and the cloud

41. What is the key responsibility of an architect in systems integration?
A. Specifying technical details for application functionality
B. Ensuring systems work together
C. Designing user interfaces
D. Writing user manuals

42. In the Dress4Win case study, which analytic platforms are suggested for processing customer data?
A. Cloud Datastore and Bigtable
B. Cloud Dataproc and BigQuery
C. Cloud SQL and Firestore
D. Cloud Spanner and Cloud Storage

43. What type of architecture is likely used by Mountkirk Games for their online games?
A. Monolithic architecture
B. Microservices architecture
C. Serverless architecture
D. Peer-to-peer architecture

44. Which service is recommended for managing APIs and securing calls to microservices?
A. Cloud Storage
B. Cloud Dataproc
C. Cloud Endpoints
D. Cloud Run

45. For TerramEarth, what is suggested to handle data ingestion from vehicles in real-time?
A. Cloud Dataflow
B. Cloud Pub/Sub

C. Cloud SQL

D. Cloud Spanner

46. What should architects consider when integrating TerramEarth and dealer systems?

A. The aesthetic design of the dealer's application

B. Significant features of the data for dealers

C. The color scheme of the user interface

D. The programming language used by dealers

47. Which storage class is recommended for data accessed once per month or less?

A. Standard storage

B. Regional storage

C. Nearline storage

D. Coldline storage

48. When planning for data management, what is a critical consideration for architects?

A. The color of the database interface

B. The expected volume of data

C. The brand of the storage hardware

D. The font used in data reports

49. What is the potential benefit of archiving data even if no immediate use is anticipated?

A. Improved user interface design

B. Better system aesthetics

C. Enhanced machine learning models

D. Reduced storage costs

50. In the context of data management, what should be developed for data stored in a database?
A. User interface guidelines
B. Data retention and deletion procedures
C. Marketing strategies
D. Branding guidelines

51. Which of the following skills are outside the scope of cloud solution design?
A. Analytical skills
B. Mechanical engineering
C. Data management
D. Predictive modeling

52. Which practice fits well with releasing incremental improvements?
A. Waterfall development
B. Agile software development
C. Big bang deployment
D. V-Model development

53. What tool can be used for collecting metrics and logging in the described solution?
A. Jenkins
B. Cloud Operations
C. Nagios
D. Prometheus

54. Which service is recommended for storing large amounts of data for analysis?
A. BigQuery

B. Cloud SQL

C. Firebase

D. Cloud Spanner

55. Which of the following is a managed relational database service on the Google Cloud Platform?

A. Cloud SQL

B. Firestore

C. Cloud Storage

D. Bigtable

56. What is the combination of all expenses related to maintaining a service called?

A. Operational expenditure

B. Capital expenditure

C. Total cost of ownership

D. Variable cost

57. Which of the following is NOT a way to reduce costs while meeting application design requirements?

A. Managed services

B. Preemptible virtual machines

C. Data lifecycle management

D. Increasing the number of on-premises servers

58. What kind of skills should be developed to better understand customer needs and equipment performance?

A. Mechanical engineering skills

B. Analytical skills

C. Financial skills

D. Marketing skills

59. What is a good practice after finding a feasible technical solution?
A. Immediately start optimizing for cost
B. Ignore cost considerations
C. Optimize for performance first
D. Test the solution extensively

60. When are managed services a good option?
A. When users need low-level control over resources
B. When developing a machine vision application
C. When managing databases manually
D. When there is a significant competitive advantage in resource management

61. Which Google Cloud Platform managed service is used for converting speech to text?
A. Cloud Text-to-Speech
B. Natural Language
C. Cloud Speech-to-Text
D. Translation

62. What is the primary purpose of Memorystore in data lifecycle management?
A. Long-term archival storage
B. Cache data for quick access
C. Store structured data
D. Provide data warehousing solutions

63. Which service is NOT NOT suitable for running applications that require high availability?

A. Bigtable
B. Preemptible VMs
C. Cloud SQL
D. Cloud Spanner

64. Which managed service would you use for creating machine learning models for structured data?
A. Cloud Inference API
B. Cloud AutoML
C. AutoML Tables
D. Dataflow

65. Which Google Cloud Platform service is used for data integration and ETL?
A. Cloud Data Fusion
B. Data Catalog
C. Cloud Pub/Sub
D. Cloud Composer

66. What action can Cloud Storage's lifecycle management feature perform on objects?
A. Encrypt the object
B. Delete an object or change its storage class
C. Compress the object
D. Duplicate the object

67. Which storage option should be used for data that is accessed at most once a year?
A. Multiregional storage
B. Regional storage

C. Nearline storage

D. Coldline storage

68. What is the purpose of Cloud Memorystore?

A. Store large amounts of unstructured data

B. Provide managed cache service using Redis

C. Manage metadata

D. Perform stream and batch processing

69. Which managed service would you use for interactive data analysis based on Jupyter Notebooks?

A. BigQuery

B. Cloud Datalab

C. Google Data Studio

D. Cloud Dataprep

70. Which of the following is a global relational database service provided by Google Cloud Platform?

A. Cloud SQL

B. Cloud Spanner

C. Bigtable

D. Cloud Data Transfer

71. Which of the following factors affects the time it takes to read and write data in a cloud environment?

A. Type of database used

B. Distance between the location of stored data and services that will process the data

C. The programming language used

D. The type of firewall applied

72. When considering stream processing, which of the following is a common practice?
A. Ignoring data older than a specified time
B. Encrypting all data in transit
C. Using batch processing techniques
D. Ensuring data is available in multiple regions

73. Which regulation addresses the privacy security of medical information in the United States?
A. GDPR
B. HIPAA
C. PCI DSS
D. COPPA

74. What is a primary tool for protecting data integrity?
A. Data replication
B. Access controls
C. Firewalls
D. Data encryption

75. What should you consider when moving from batch processing to stream processing?
A. The type of hardware used
B. The programming language used
C. The volume of data
D. How to deal with late arriving and missing data

76. Which regulation specifies security controls to protect cardholders' data?
A. HIPAA
B. GDPR
C. PCI DSS

D. SOX

77. What is a common way to protect data during its lifecycle?
A. Encrypting data at rest and in motion
B. Using batch processing
C. Keeping data on-premises
D. Regularly deleting old data

78. Which concept assumes that any security control may be compromised, so systems should be protected with multiple types of controls?
A. Single point of failure
B. Least privilege
C. Defense in depth
D. Role-based access control

79. What does ROI stand for, and how is it expressed?
A. Return on Investment, expressed as a percentage
B. Rate of Interest, expressed as a decimal
C. Return on Income, expressed as a ratio
D. Rate of Increase, expressed as a fraction

80. What is a KPI, and why is it important in the context of cloud projects?
A. Key Process Improvement: it helps in process optimization
B. Key Performance Indicator: it helps measure the success of a project
C. Knowledge Performance Index: it evaluates employee knowledge
D. Key Product Innovation: it tracks new product developments

81. What is the allowed downtime per day for a service with a 99.99% availability SLA?
A. 14.4 minutes
B. 1.44 minutes

C. 8.64 seconds

D. 864 milliseconds

82. Which of the following is NOT a method to compensate for hardware failures?

A. Writing data to multiple disks

B. Using a single server to reduce complexity

C. Creating instance groups with multiple servers

D. Installing two direct network connections with different vendors

83. What is the purpose of a managed instance group in Compute Engine?

A. To create a single VM with a unique configuration

B. To maintain multiple VMs with different configurations

C. To create a cluster of VMs with the same configuration

D. To ensure VMs operate without any configuration templates

84. Which high availability feature allows VMs to be moved to other physical servers during maintenance?

A. Auto-healing

B. Live migration

C. Regional instance groups

D. Global load balancing

85. What is the primary benefit of using global load balancing in GCP?

A. It reduces the need, for instance templates

B. It ensures application availability across multiple regions

C. It eliminates the need for regional instance groups

D. It increases the complexity of application deployment

86. In Kubernetes Engine, what is the smallest unit of deployment called?
A. Node
B. Container
C. Pod
D. Cluster

87. Which feature in managed instance groups helps address application-level failures?
A. Live migration
B. Auto-healing
C. Global load balancing
D. Regional instance groups

88. Which of the following is a fully managed compute service in GCP?
A. Compute Engine
B. Kubernetes Engine
C. App Engine
D. Managed instances, groups,

89. What is the key advantage of creating a regional cluster in Kubernetes Engine?
A. Reduced deployment time
B. Increased configuration complexity
C. Distribution of VMs across multiple zones
D. Single-zone deployment simplicity

90. Which of the following downtime amounts is allowed for a service with a 99.999% availability SLA per month?
A. 26.3 seconds
B. 2.63 seconds

C. 4.38 minutes
D. 43.83 minutes

91. Which of the following storage options meets the requirement to "dynamically scale up or down based on game activity" for Mountkirk Games?
A. Cloud SQL
B. Bigtable
C. BigQuery
D. Cloud Spanner

92. What is a key benefit of using regional replication in Bigtable?
A. Reduces storage costs
B. Provides autoscaling
C. Improves availability
D. Increases network speed

93. Which networking option should be considered if global network availability is a concern?
A. Standard Network Tier
B. Premium Network Tier
C. VPN
D. Dedicated Interconnect

94. Which database storage option is suitable for storing 9 TB of time-series data per day for TerramEarth?
A. Cloud SQL
B. Bigtable
C. Cloud Spanner
D. Cloud Storage

95. What is the main advantage of using redundant network connections between an on-premises data center and Google's data center?
A. Reduces latency
B. Increases network availability
C. Decreases security risks
D. Lowers costs

96. Which Google Cloud service is recommended for storing images, logs, and backups for Dress4Win?
A. Cloud SQL
B. Bigtable
C. Cloud Storage
D. Cloud Spanner

97. What is a primary consideration when using regional persistent disks with Compute Engine VMs?
A. Cost reduction
B. Increased availability
C. Improved network speed
D. Enhanced security

98. Which tool should be used to monitor the state of applications and detect problems early?
A. Cloud Pub/Sub
B. Cloud Dataflow
C. Cloud Operations Monitoring
D. Cloud Storage

99. What is one of the primary ways to improve network availability?
A. Using a single network connection

B. Using Standard Tier networking

C. Using redundant network connections

D. Reducing data transmission

100. What is the primary challenge in scaling stateful applications horizontally?

A. Lack of sufficient VM instances

B. Difficulty in distributing state information across instances

C. High cost of additional storage

D. Complexity in deploying additional network interconnects

101. Which Google Cloud Platform service allows you to run small functions in response to events without setting up and managing servers?

A. Compute Engine

B. App Engine

C. Cloud Functions

D. Kubernetes Engine

102. What type of virtual machine (VM) in the Google Cloud Platform has balanced CPU and memory allocations?

A. Highmem instances

B. High CPU instances

C. Standard instances

D. Ulramem instances

103. Which of the following is a managed Kubernetes service offered by Google Cloud Platform?

A. Cloud Functions

B. Kubernetes Engine

C. App Engine

D. Compute Engine

104. What type of machine will run up to 24 hours and can be shut down by GCP at any time?
A. Standard VM
B. Managed instance
C. Preemptible VM
D. Shielded VM

105. Which feature of Shielded VMs verifies all boot components using UEFI firmware features?
A. Secure boot
B. vTPM
C. Integrity monitoring
D. Sole tenancy

106. What is the primary purpose of a service account associated with a VM?
A. To manage network interfaces
B. To encrypt data
C. To perform actions on behalf of the VM
D. To specify boot images

107. Which of the following types of disks can be specified when creating a VM boot image?
A. Local SSD
B. Persistent disk
C. SSD persistent disk
D. All of the above

108. What should you select if you need to ensure that your VMs run only on physical servers with other VMs from the same project?
A. Shielded VM
B. Preemptible VM
C. Sole tenancy
D. Managed instance group

109. What is the difference between managed and unmanaged instance groups in GCP?
A. Managed instance groups contain identical VMs. Unmanaged ones do not.
B. Unmanaged instance groups are used for new configurations.
C. Managed instance groups are not provisioned using an instance template.
D. Unmanaged instance groups are recommended for new configurations.

110. What kind of boot image can you NOT specify when creating a VM?
A. Predefined boot images
B. Custom boot images based on predefined ones
C. Boot images with no encryption
D. Boot images with SSD persistent disks

111. Which of the following languages is NOT supported in the first-generation App Engine Standard?
A. Python 2.7
B. Java 8
C. PHP 5.5
D. Python 3.7

112. What network access restriction applies to Python 2.7, PHP 5.5, and Go 1.9 in the first-generation App Engine Standard?

A. No network access

B. Full network access

C. Only through a URL Fetch API

D. Only through a VPN

113. Which App Engine environment is recommended for applications that need to scale rapidly up or down depending on traffic?

A. App Engine Standard

B. App Engine Flexible

C. Compute Engine

D. Kubernetes Engine

114. What is the default instance startup time for App Engine Flexible?

A. Seconds

B. Minutes

C. Hours

D. Days

115. Which service is better suited for a publish/subscribe-type messaging service in a GCP environment?

A. App Engine Task Queues

B. Cloud Pub/Sub

C. Compute Engine

D. Kubernetes Engine

116. Which of the following is NOT a supported runtime in App Engine Flexible by default?

A. Java 8

B. Python 2.7

C. Ruby

D. Java 11

117. How often are containers in App Engine Flexible restarted?
A. Daily
B. Weekly
C. Monthly
D. Annually

118. Which component of Kubernetes is responsible for determining where to run pods?
A. Controller manager
B. API server
C. Scheduler
D. etcd

119. What is the primary disadvantage of a complete deployment?
A. It updates all instances of the modified code at once.
B. It requires a single server running a monolithic application.
C. It introduces the risk of problematic code to all users at once.
D. It uses two production environments, named Blue and Green.

120. In Kubernetes, which abstraction provides a stable API endpoint and stable IP address for applications?
A. Pod
B. Service
C. ReplicaSet
D. Deployment

121. What object in Kubernetes is responsible for controlling external access to services running in a cluster?

A. ReplicaSet
B. StatefulSet
C. PersistentVolume
D. Ingress

122. What is the purpose of a PersistentVolumeClaim in Kubernetes?
A. To manage stateful applications
B. To link a pod to persistent storage
C. To control external access to pods
D. To monitor the health of pods

123. Which compute service on the Google Cloud Platform is well-suited for event processing?
A. Kubernetes Engine
B. App Engine Flexible
C. Cloud Functions
D. Compute Engine

124. Which of the following events can Cloud Functions respond to?
A. HTTP GET, POST, PUT, DELETE, OPTIONS
B. Kubernetes Pod Creation
C. App Engine Deployments
D. Virtual Machine Shutdown

125. What is a StatefulSet in Kubernetes used for?
A. To manage stateless applications
B. To assign unique identifiers to stateful pods
C. To link pods to persistent storage
D. To control external access to services

126. In which programming languages can Cloud Functions currently be written?
A. Java, Python, Go
B. Python 3, Go, Node.js 8 and 10
C. C++, Java, Python
D. Ruby, PHP, Python

127. Which Kubernetes object ensures the desired number of pod replicas are running?
A. Ingress
B. PersistentVolume
C. ReplicaSet
D. StatefulSet

128. What is the primary use case for Google Cloud's Deployment Manager?
A. To manage Kubernetes clusters
B. To define infrastructure as code
C. To execute serverless functions
D. To handle stateful applications

129. Which of the following is a use case for Cloud Functions?
A. Running containers
B. Managing Kubernetes clusters
C. Responding to events like file uploads
D. Creating virtual machines

130. What platform does Kubernetes Engine provide for deploying applications?
A. Virtual Machines
B. Serverless Functions

C. Containerized Services

D. Database Triggers

131. What is a common issue when assigning sensors to instances based on machine ID in a stateful system?

A. It evenly distributes the workload across all instances.

B. Some servers may have significantly more load than others.

C. It requires fewer compute resources.

D. It eliminates the need for state information.

132. What is one approach to handle instance volatility in stateful systems?

A. Using only synchronous operations.

B. Storing state data in volatile instances.

C. Moving state data to a separate data store.

D. Assigning more sensors to fewer instances.

133. Which of the following is a managed Redis service suitable for low-latency access to data?

A. Cloud SQL

B. Cloud Datastore

C. Cloud Memorystore

D. Cloud Pub/Sub

134. What is a potential disadvantage of using databases to store state data in stateful systems?

A. They always provide lower latency than caches.

B. They do not persist data to durable storage.

C. They can be complex to maintain and tune.

D. They cannot be used with managed services.

135. Why might asynchronous operations be preferred over synchronous operations in certain workflows?
A. They always complete faster than synchronous operations.
B. They can decouple immediate and later work, reducing delays.
C. They require less computing resources.
D. They are easier to implement.

136. Which GCP service is recommended for buffering data between services and supports both push and pull subscriptions?
A. Cloud SQL
B. Cloud Datastore
C. Cloud Dataflow
D. Cloud Pub/Sub

137. What is the primary benefit of using a message queue in a workflow?
A. It eliminates the need for any form of synchronization.
B. It ensures data is always processed in real-time.
C. It helps buffer data between services, managing load effectively.
D. It reduces the overall latency of the system.

138. In the context of monitoring and alerting, what is meant by "actionable alerts"?
A. Alerts that require immediate manual intervention.
B. Alerts that provide enough information to correct the problem.
C. Alerts that are automatically logged.
D. Alerts that are ignored until a critical threshold is reached

139. Which GCP service is a fully managed implementation of the Apache Beam stream processing framework?
A. Cloud SQL

B. Cloud Datastore

C. Cloud Dataflow

D. Cloud Memorystore

140. What should be considered when designing workflows to meet business requirements?

A. Only the compute resources are needed.

B. How data will flow from one service to the next.

C. The number of sensors in use.

D. The type of database used.

141. What is an instance template in Google Cloud?

A. A template for creating Kubernetes clusters

B. A template for managing disk encryption keys

C. A template defining properties of a VM

D. A template for developing applications in Python

142. What is one of the primary benefits of using Managed Instance Groups (MIGs)?

A. Reduced cost of operation

B. Manual updates

C. Autohealing using application health checks

D. Limited scalability

143. Which of the following is a use case for a Compute Engine?

A. Running serverless applications without configuring servers

B. Implementing Kubernetes clusters

C. Running stateful applications like databases

D. Using predefined machine learning models

144. What feature allows MIGs to test a new version of instance templates before deploying it across the group?
A. Rolling updates
B. Autohealing
C. Canary updates
D. Load balancing

145. In which of the following scenarios is App Engine Standard a suitable choice?
A. Running custom containers with high IOPS
B. Running serverless applications with specific language support
C. Managing disk encryption keys
D. Implementing advanced container orchestration

146. What is the default instance class for applications running in App Engine Standard?
A. F1
B. B3
C. A2
D. D1

147. Which Google Cloud service would you use if you need to manage your disk encryption keys?
A. Kubernetes Engine
B. Compute Engine
C. App Engine Flexible
D. Cloud Storage

148. Which type of persistent disk should you configure for high Input/Output Operations Per Second (IOPS) in the Compute Engine?
A. Standard persistent disks

B. SSD persistent disks

C. HDD persistent disks

D. Temporary persistent disks

149. What is a key feature of App Engine Flexible?

A. It supports only a limited set of programming languages

B. It allows running custom containers in a platform-as-a-service

C. It requires manual scaling of instances

D. It is strictly for batch-processing jobs

150. Which Google Cloud service should be used if you prefer advanced container-orchestration features?

A. App Engine Standard

B. Compute Engine

C. Kubernetes Engine

D. Cloud Functions

151. What type of data is Google Cloud Storage most suitable for?

A. Structured data

B. Unstructured data

C. Relational databases

D. Block storage data

152. Which of the following is NOT a best practice for naming buckets in Google Cloud Storage?

A. Using DNS naming conventions

B. Using globally unique identifiers (GUIDs)

C. Using personally identifying information

D. Avoiding sequential names or timestamps

153. What is the key difference between Regional and Multiregional storage types?
A. Regional storage is cheaper than Multiregional storage.
B. Multiregional storage stores copies of objects in multiple regions.
C. Regional storage has better availability than Multiregional storage.
D. Multiregional storage offers less durability than Regional storage.

154. In a rolling deployment, how is the deployment process typically executed?
A. All servers are updated simultaneously.
B. A deployment is released to one server at a time over a period.
C. Only one environment is used for deployment.
D. New code is released without routing any traffic initially.

155. Which of the following storage classes has the highest availability SLA in multiregional locations?
A. Regional storage
B. Multiregional storage
C. Nearline storage
D. Coldline storage

156. Which tool allows you to mount Google Cloud Storage buckets as filesystems on Linux and MacOS platforms?
A. gsutil
B. Cloud Console
C. Cloud Storage FUSE
D. Compute Engine

157. What is the primary use case for Nearline storage?
A. Frequently accessed data
B. Data accessed less than once in 30 days.

C. Real-time analytics

D. Temporary storage

158. Which of the following is NOT a characteristic of Google Cloud Storage?

A. It provides high durability with eleven 9s (99.999999999%) annual durability.

B. It supports hierarchical directory structures natively.

C. It treats objects as atomic units.

D. It provides multiple storage tiers

159. Which of the following is a valid use case for Google Cloud Storage?

A. Running transactional databases

B. Storing and sharing log files among multiple instances

C. Hosting a web server

D. Real-time data processing

160. What is the primary benefit of using Multiregional storage over Regional storage?

A. Lower cost

B. Higher durability

C. Improved access times and latency

D. Higher availability in regional locations

161. What are the two tiers of Google Cloud Filestore?

A. Basic and Standard

B. Standard and Premium

C. Silver and Gold

D. Economy and Deluxe

162. Which of the following is a typical use case for Cloud Filestore?
A. Video streaming
B. Web server content
C. Cryptocurrency mining
D. Real-time analytics

163. What is the maximum read throughput for a 10+ TB Premium Cloud Filestore?
A. 100 MB/s
B. 180 MB/s
C. 1.2 GB/s
D. 2.5 GB/s

164. Which IAM role grants administrative permissions to create and delete Cloud Filestore instances?
A. Cloud Filestore User
B. Cloud Filestore Viewer
C. Cloud Filestore Admin
D. Cloud Filestore Editor

165. Which relational database service is described as supporting horizontal scalability across regions?
A. Cloud SQL
B. Cloud Spanner
C. Bigtable
D. Firestore

166. Which ACID property ensures that once a transaction is executed, the state of the database will always reflect that change?
A. Atomicity
B. Consistency

C. Isolation

D. Durability

167. What is a key feature of Cloud SQL?

A. Support for non-relational databases

B. Data is not encrypted.

C. Data replication across multiple zones

D. Requires manual patching

168. Which of the following is NOT a typical use case for Cloud Spanner?

A. Financial trading systems

B. Logistics applications

C. Video streaming services

D. Global inventory tracking

169. What is the typical availability percentage for both the Standard and Premium tiers of Cloud Filestore?

A. 99.5 percent

B. 99.9 percent

C. 99.99 percent

D. 100 percent

170. What is the main advantage of using Cloud CDN?

A. It supports flexible data models

B. It provides real-time updates

C. It reduces latency by caching static content at edge nodes

D. It manages data retention policies

171. Which of the following is a managed data warehouse and analytics database solution in GCP?

A. Cloud SQL

B. Cloud Spanner

C. BigQuery

D. Cloud Datastore

172. What is the purpose of the 'bq head' command in BigQuery?

A. Insert data in newline JSON format

B. List the first rows of a table

C. Create a job to run a SQL query

D. Delete objects

173. Which of the following roles in BigQuery allows a user to perform all operations on BigQuery resources?

A. data viewer

B. jobUser

C. admin

D. metadata viewer

174. For which type of data organization does BigQuery use a columnar format?

A. To store data from the same row together

B. To store values from a single column together

C. To store values from a single dataset together

D. To store values from a single table together

175. What is the primary use of Cloud Bigtable?

A. Transaction processing systems

B. Streaming Internet of Things (IoT) data

C. Data warehousing

D. Document storage

176. Which of the following is NOT supported by Cloud Datastore?

A. ACID transactions

B. Strong consistency for lookup by key

C. Joins

D. SQL-like query language called GQL

177. What is the benefit of using BigQuery's --dry-run option for command-line queries?

A. It inserts data from AVRO, CSV, ORC, Parquet, and JSON data files

B. It returns an estimate of the number of bytes that would be returned if the query were executed

C. It lists the first rows of a table

D. It stops a job

178. What type of database is Cloud Spanner?

A. NoSQL database

B. Document database

C. Relational database

D. Analytics database

179. How does BigQuery charge for its services?

A. Based on the number of queries run

B. Based on the amount of data stored and the amount of data scanned

C. Based on the number of datasets created

D. Based on the number of users accessing the data

180. Which command would you use in BigQuery to create a new table, view, or dataset?

A. mk

B. insert

C. query

D. show

181. What is the primary function of a Virtual Private Cloud (VPC. in Google Cloud Platform (GCP)?
A. Manage billing and access controls based on identities
B. Organize Compute Engine instances, App Engine Flexible instances, and GKE clusters
C. Create machine learning models
D. Monitor application performance

182. Which of the following is NOT a characteristic of a VPC subnet?
A. Must have distinct IP address ranges
B. Can span multiple regions
C. Provides private addresses to resources in the region
D. Can be automatically created with IP ranges based on the region

183. What is the advantage of using VPC network peering?
A. Higher egress charges
B. Increased latency due to public Internet conditions
C. Reduced attack surface as services are inaccessible from the public Internet
D. Requirement of external IP addresses

184. What is the purpose of a Shared VPC?
A. To manage billing for multiple projects
B. To allow communication between resources in different projects
C. To create automatic subnets for each region
D. To enforce firewall rules globally

185. What is one of the implied firewall rules associated with VPCs?
A. Allow all incoming traffic
B. Block all outgoing traffic
C. Allow all outgoing traffic
D. Block all internal traffic

186. What is the key difference between VPC peering and Shared VPC?
A. VPC peering can connect VPCs within the same organization only
B. Shared VPC can connect VPCs between different organizations
C. VPC peering can connect VPCs between different organizations
D. Shared VPC does not allow resource communication

187. How many default firewall rules are assigned to the default network in a VPC?
A. Two
B. Four
C. Six
D. Eight

188. What priority value would you assign to a firewall rule to override the implied rules?
A. 65535
B. 0
C. Any value greater than 65535
D. Any value less than 65535

189. Which of the following is a benefit of using Shared VPCs?
A. Increased latency
B. Complex network management
C. Separation of project and network management duties
D. Higher egress charges

190. What is a primary advantage of VPC network peering over using external IP addresses?
A. Higher latency due to external routing
B. Lower egress charges
C. Increased attack surface
D. Dependency on public Internet conditions

191. Which protocol is used by the default-allow-rdp firewall rule to allow ingress connections?
A. SSH
B. ICMP
C. TCP
D. UDP

192. What is the priority value assigned to the default firewall rules mentioned?
A. 100
B. 65534
C. 1
D. 50000

193. Which attribute of a firewall rule specifies whether the traffic direction is inbound or outbound?
A. Action
B. Direction
C. Protocol
D. Target

194. What does CIDR stand for in networking?
A. Classless Inter-Domain Routing
B. Cloud Inter-Domain Routing
C. Classful Internet Domain Routing
D. Circuit Inter-Domain Routing

195. Which hybrid-cloud network topology involves the public cloud and private on-premise environments mirroring each other?
A. Meshed topology
B. Gated egress topology
C. Mirrored topology
D. Handover topology

196. For which type of workload is a hybrid-cloud environment particularly recommended?
A. A web application with low-traffic
B. Batch processing jobs using legacy applications
C. Static website hosting
D. Simple database queries

197. Which hybrid-cloud network topology ensures that on-premises service APIs are available to cloud applications without exposing them to the public Internet?
A. Meshed topology
B. Gated egress topology
C. Handover topology
D. Gated ingress topology

198. IPv4 addresses use how many octets?
A. Two octets
B. Three octets

C. Four octets

D. Eight octets

199. What is the primary concern when using a single network interconnect in a hybrid-cloud environment?

A. Cost

B. Complexity

C. Latency

D. Single point of failure

200. What does the integer in a CIDR block represent?

A. The number of available IP addresses

B. The number of subnets

C. The number of bits used to identify the subnet

D. The number of regions in the VPC

201. Which type of network link provides virtual private networks between GCP and on-premises networks using IPsec VPNs?

A. Cloud VPN

B. Cloud Interconnect

C. Direct Peering

D. HTTP(S) Load Balancing

202. What is the primary advantage of using Cloud Interconnect over Cloud VPN?

A. Lower cost

B. Transmission of data on private connections

C. Simplicity of management

D. Support for up to 3 Gbps bandwidth

203. Which load balancer should you use if you need to distribute HTTP and HTTPS traffic globally?
A. Network TCP/UDP
B. Internal TCP/UDP
C. HTTP(S) Load Balancing
D. SSL Proxy Load Balancing

204. Which type of load balancer is specifically designed to handle non-HTTPS and non-SSL traffic globally?
A. Network TCP/UDP
B. Internal TCP/UDP
C. HTTP(S) Load Balancing
D. TCP Proxy Load Balancing

205. What encryption protocol does Cloud VPN use to protect data in transit?
A. SSL/TLS
B. BGP
C. IKE
D. HTTPS

206. Which network link option is recommended primarily when low latency and high availability are not required?
A. Cloud Interconnect
B. Cloud VPN
C. Direct Peering
D. Network TCP/UDP Load Balancer

207. What is one of the disadvantages of using Cloud Interconnect?
A. It has a lower bandwidth than Cloud VPN.
B. It requires additional cost and complexity to manage.

C. It uses public IP addresses for data transmission.

D. It cannot scale up to higher bandwidths.

208. Which load balancer is the appropriate choice for distributing the workload across backend services running on Compute Engine instances with private IP addresses?

A. Network TCP/UDP Load Balancer

B. Internal TCP/UDP Load Balancer

C. HTTP(S) Load Balancer

D. SSL Proxy Load Balancer

209. What advantage does the SSL Proxy Load Balancer provide for backend instances?

A. It offloads SSL encryption/decryption.

B. It distributes HTTP and HTTPS traffic globally.

C. It supports non-SSL and non-TCP traffic.

D. It routes traffic based on URL maps.

210. Which networking option allows for routing between networks by exchanging BGP routes?

A. Cloud VPN

B. Cloud Interconnect

C. Direct Peering

D. Internal TCP/UDP Load Balancer

211. What is the main function of the Identity and Access Management (IAM) service in Google Cloud Platform (GCP)?

A. To create virtual machines

B. To specify what operations specific users can perform on particular resources

C. To manage billing and payments

D. To deploy applications

212. Which of the following is NOT a type of identity in GCP IAM?

A. Google account

B. Service account

C. Cloud Identity domain

D. Billing account

213. What kind of permissions does a user with the Viewer role have?

A. Read-only permissions

B. Write permissions

C. Administrative permissions

D. No permissions

214. What is the naming convention for predefined roles in GCP IAM?

A. service-name/role

B. permissions/roles

C. roles/service-name.role

D. role/service

215. Which type of IAM role allows the creation of custom permissions tailored to specific needs?

A. Primitive roles

B. Predefined roles

C. Custom roles

D. Service roles

216. Which of the following is a permission associated with Compute Engine?

A. storage.objects.create

B. compute.instances.get

C. bigquery.datasets.create

D. pubsub.subscriptions.consume

217. Service accounts are primarily used by:

A. Applications running in GCP

B. Billing departments

C. External contractors

D. Human resource departments

218. Which role should be granted to a user who needs to manage roles and permissions for a resource?

A. Viewer

B. Editor

C. Owner

D. Admin

219. What is a Google Group in the context of IAM?

A. A type of identity used to perform actions on GCP resources

B. A set of Google accounts and service accounts

C. A billing management entity

D. A cloud storage container

220. Which IAM role is suitable for a user who needs to query a database but not administer it?

A. roles/bigquery.dataEditor

B. roles/bigquery.admin

C. roles/cloudsql.viewer

D. roles/bigquery.user

221. Which of the following principles is followed by ensuring that a user has the fewest permissions possible to perform their tasks?
A. Principle of Maximum Security
B. Principle of Least Privilege
C. Principle of Role-Based Access
D. Principle of User Management

222. What is the role 'roles/cloudfunctions.developer' used for?
A. Managing Cloud Storage Buckets
B. Viewing and setting Cloud Functions source code
C. Administering IAM roles and policies
D. Monitoring Cloud Audit Logs

223. If a developer should only be able to view the source code but not change it, what should be done?
A. Grant the role 'roles/cloudfunctions.admin'
B. Create a custom role excluding 'cloudfunctions.functions.sourceCodeSet.'
C. Assign 'roles/storage.objectViewer' role
D. Grant the role 'roles/cloudfunctions.viewer.'

224. What format is used to specify policies in Google Cloud IAM?
A. XML
B. YAML
C. JSON
D. CSV

225. Which function of the Cloud IAM API is used to set policies on resources?
A. get a policy
B. setIamPolicy

C. testIamPermissions

D. updateIamPolicy

226. Where can policies be set in the Google Cloud Platform resource hierarchy?

A. At the organization, folder, or project level only

B. Only at the project level

C. At any level, including individual resources

D. Only at the organizational level

227. What is an effective way to manage multiple roles needed to perform a task?

A. Assign roles individually to each user

B. Grant broad permissions to all users

C. Grant roles to a group and add users to the group

D. Use primitive roles for all users

228. What should be reviewed to monitor changes to IAM policies?

A. Cloud SQL logs

B. Cloud Storage access logs

C. Cloud Audit Logs

D. Cloud Functions logs

229. Google Cloud encrypts data at rest by default using which encryption standards?

A. DES and RSA

B. AES256 and AES128

C. MD5 and SHA-1

D. Blowfish and Twofish

230. What is 'envelope encryption' in the context of Google Cloud's data security?
A. Encrypting data with a single key
B. Encrypting the data encryption keys with another key
C. Using envelopes to store encryption keys
D. Encrypting data at rest only

231. What type of encryption is used by new storage devices in Google Cloud Platform (GCP)?
A. AES128
B. AES192
C. AES256
D. RSA2048

232. What is the role of the Google Front End in GCP?
A. Encrypting data at rest
B. Managing encryption keys
C. Terminating HTTP and HTTPS traffic and routing it over the Google network
D. Scanning for vulnerabilities

233. Which protocol does GCP use for encryption in transit within its infrastructure?
A. TLS
B. QUICK
C. ALTS
D. IPsec

234. How does Google Cloud manage Data Encryption Keys (DEKs) by default?
A. DEKs are stored in the application server

B. DEKs are stored near the data chunks they encrypt

C. DEKs are stored in an on-premises server

D. DEKs are stored in the client's local machine

235. What is a primary feature of Cloud KMS in GCP?

A. It allows customers to generate and store keys on-premises

B. It is a third-party key management service

C. It enables customers to generate and store keys in GCP

D. It does not support AES256

236. Which of the following key management methods provides the most control to the customer?

A. Default Key Management

B. Cloud KMS

C. Customer-Supplied Keys

D. Google Managed Keys

237. What is the delay period before a Cloud KMS key is destroyed after a deletion request?

A. Immediate

B. 24 hours

C. 48 hours

D. One week

238. What is the first phase of a penetration test, according to the text?

A. Scanning

B. Gaining access

C. Reconnaissance

D. Maintaining access

239. Which phase of penetration testing involves attackers hiding their presence?

A. Scanning

B. Gaining access

C. Maintaining access

D. Removing footprints

240. How is data in transit on the public Internet treated by GCP?

A. It is authenticated but not encrypted

B. It is neither authenticated nor encrypted

C. It is encrypted

D. It is encrypted only if requested by the user

241. What must you comply with when conducting a penetration test on Google Cloud Platform (GCP)?

A. Notify Google before starting the test

B. Comply with the terms of service for GCP

C. Use only Google-approved tools

D. Perform the test only during non-business hours

242. Which of the following services can collect logs from widely used services like Jenkins, MySQL, and Redis?

A. Cloud Audit Logs

B. Cloud Pub/Sub

C. Cloud Operations Logging Agent

D. Cloud Storage

243. What is the purpose of Cloud Audit Logs in GCP?

A. To automatically fix configuration errors

B. To record administrative actions and data operations

C. To store backup data

D. To provide a firewall for network security

244. How can logs be exported from Cloud Operations?
A. Direct email to administrators
B. XML files to a local server
C. JSON files to Cloud Storage
D. CSV files to Google Sheets

245. What is one of the security design principles in cloud architecture?
A. Unlimited privileges
B. Centralized duties
C. Least privilege
D. Single point of failure

246. In the context of separation of duties, what is a typical example in a finance department?
A. One person both creates and pays bills
B. A single person approves all financial transactions
C. One person creates a bill, and another pays it
D. The same person manages all financial records

247. What role in App Engine can read, write, and modify access to all application configurations and settings?
A. roles/appengine.appViewer
B. roles/appengine.codeViewer
C. roles/appengine.deployer
D. roles/appengine.appadmin

248. Which practice involves using more than one security control to protect resources and data?

A. Least Privilege
B. Defense in Depth
C. Separation of Duties
D. Centralized Management

249. What should you do to meet regulations that require audit logs to be retained for longer periods?
A. Delete logs after one month
B. Export audit logs from Cloud Audit Logs to Cloud Storage or BigQuery
C. Keep logs only in Cloud Operations
D. Use only manual logging methods

250. Which IAM role is NOT suitable for implementing the principle of least privilege due to its broad permissions?
A. roles/appengine.appViewer
B. roles/viewer
C. roles/app engine.code viewer
D. roles/app engine.service admin

251. Which of the following is an example of a phishing attack consequence?
A. Loss of physical infrastructure
B. Coaxing a user's login credentials
C. Enforcing firewall rules
D. Implementing GDPR

252. What is the primary method to prevent an attacker from accessing resources after a phishing attack?
A. Disabling firewalls
B. Allowing traffic from any IP address

C. Implementing trusted IP address rules

D. Using open-source software

253. Which widely used open-source cryptographic software library was found vulnerable due to Heartbleed in 2014?

A. Microsoft Azure

B. Google Cloud Platform

C. OpenSSL

D. Apache HTTP Server

254. What is the primary goal of regulations like HIPAA/HITECH and GDPR?

A. Increase sales of cloud services

B. Protect privacy and ensure information security

C. Reduce the cost of IT infrastructure

D. Promote open-source software

255. Who is responsible for application-level security in Google Cloud Platform (GCP)?

A. Google

B. The ISP

C. GCP customers

D. Software vendors

256. Under HIPAA, what rights do patients have regarding their healthcare records?

A. No rights

B. The right to edit their records

C. The right to review and request information

D. The right to delete their records

257. What does the HIPAA Security Rule require organizations to ensure?
A. Unlimited data sharing
B. Confidentiality, integrity, and availability of healthcare information
C. Free access to all healthcare data
D. Use of only proprietary software

258. When was the Health Information Technology for Economic and Clinical Health (HITECH) Act enacted?
A. 1996
B. 2003
C. 2009
D. 2014

259. Which regulation applies to individuals living in the European Union?
A. HIPAA
B. HITECH
C. SOX
D. GDPR

260. What should organizations have in place according to the HIPAA Security Rule?
A. A firewall and antivirus software
B. Security management practices, access control practices, incident response procedures, and contingency planning
C. A single security officer
D. Unlimited internet access

261. Which of the following Google Cloud services is NOT covered under Google's Business Associate Agreement (BAA. for HIPAA) compliance?

A. Compute Engine

B. App Engine

C. Kubernetes Engine

D. None of the above

262. Under the GDPR, who is responsible for gaining and managing the consent of individuals whose data is collected?

A. Processor

B. Controller

C. Supervising authority

D. Data Protection Officer

263. What action must data processors take in the event of a data breach under GDPR?

A. Notify the controller

B. Notify the supervising authority

C. Notify the individuals whose data was compromised

D. Notify the general public

264. The Sarbanes-Oxley Act (SOX) was enacted to protect the public from fraudulent accounting practices in which type of companies?

A. Private companies

B. Publicly traded companies

C. Non-profit organizations

D. Government agencies

265. Which of the following is NOT a requirement under the Children's Online Privacy Protection Act (COPPA)?

A. Post clear and comprehensive privacy policies

B. Provide direct notice to parents before collecting a child's personal information

C. Give parents the opportunity to block collection of a child's data

D. Encrypt all collected data

266. Which of the following is NOT part of ITIL's general management practices?

A. Strategy

B. Architecture

C. Incident management

D. Risk management

267. Under SOX, companies are required to implement what type of controls to protect financial data?

A. Physical controls

B. Access controls

C. Biometric controls

D. Logical controls

268. What is the primary focus of the Children's Online Privacy Protection Act (COPPA)?

A. Protecting children's health information

B. Protecting children's education records

C. Protecting children's online privacy

D. Protecting children's financial data

269. Which of the following is a reason an organization may adopt the ITIL framework?

A. To comply with HIPAA regulations

B. To establish repeatable good practices

C. To encrypt data

D. To manage financial records

270. Which of the following is NOT a practice area under ITIL?
A. General management practices
B. Service management practices
C. Technical management practices
D. Financial management practices

271. What is the primary purpose of Cloud Operations Monitoring?
A. To collect service-specific details about operations
B. To notify responsible parties about issues with applications or infrastructure
C. To collect measurements of key aspects of infrastructure and applications
D. To automate application deployment

272. Which of the following is NOT a component of Cloud Operations?
A. Monitoring
B. Logging
C. Alerting
D. Deployment

273. What is a "time series" in the context of Cloud Operations Monitoring?
A. A graph of all metrics
B. A set of metrics recorded with a time stamp
C. A type of alerting policy
D. A script for automating tasks

274. What can be inferred if the cache hit ratio is dropping for an application?
A. The database is performing faster.
B. The application does not need a cache.

C. The memory size is no longer sufficient to meet the needs of the service.

D. The application is using less CPU.

275. What is the goal of alerting in Cloud Operations?

A. To automate the scaling of resources

B. To notify someone when there is an incident that cannot be automatically remediated

C. To improve code quality

D. To deploy new versions of applications

276. What should be done to prevent receiving too many false alerts in Cloud Operations?

A. Set very low threshold values

B. Ignore all alerts

C. Find an optimal threshold through experimentation

D. Disable alerting

277. In the context of Cloud Operations Monitoring, what is a metric?

A. A rule for alerting

B. A visual display of data

C. A measurement of a key aspect of infrastructure or applications

D. A type of notification

278. Which of the following is an example of how dashboards can be useful?

A. Automating service deployment

B. Identifying correlated failures

C. Writing code

D. Setting up network configurations

279. What is the role of conditions in Cloud Operations alerting policies?
A. To define the format of logs
B. To set rules for when a resource is in an unhealthy state
C. To deploy application updates
D. To measure application performance

280. How can Cloud Operations Monitoring help in maintaining cost-efficient services?
A. By reducing the need for human intervention
B. By automatically scaling resources up and down
C. By providing detailed data about the state of applications and infrastructure
D. By automating code quality checks

281. What is "alert fatigue" in the context of system monitoring?
A. The condition where there are so many unnecessary alerts that engineers are less likely to pay attention to them.
B. The state of being tired from working long hours.
C. The point at which an alert system stops functioning.
D. The condition where alerts are not sent at all.

282. How can reliability be improved in Compute Engine?
A. By ignoring alerts.
B. By manually responding to changes in workload.
C. By automatically responding to changes in workload or other conditions.
D. By running more VMs without load balancing.

283. What is one advantage of using managed services like BigQuery over running a relational database in Compute Engine?
A. It is cheaper.
B. It eliminates the need to monitor servers.
C. It provides better performance.

D. It requires fewer engineers.

284. What is a key feature of Cloud Operations Logging?
A. It can only store logs from GCP resources.
B. It can store logs from virtually any application or resource.
C. It doesn't support log searching.
D. It only retains logs for 7 days.

285. How long does Cloud Operations Logging retain log messages by default?
A. 7 days
B. 15 days
C. 30 days
D. 60 days

286. What can you do if you need to keep logs for longer than the default retention period in Cloud Operations Logging?
A. Delete old logs.
B. Export them to Cloud Storage or BigQuery.
C. Compress the logs.
D. Export them to a local drive.

287. Which of the following is NOT a feature of Cloud Operations Logging?
A. Text searching
B. Structured SQL-based analysis via BigQuery
C. Integration with Cloud Operations Alerting
D. Automatic bug fixing

288. What is an example of an event that might trigger a log message?
A. A user logging in successfully.
B. A database connection error.

C. An engineer starting their shift.

D. A printer running out of paper.

289. What are the three essential tools provided by Cloud Operations for observing and understanding the state of services?

A. Monitoring, alerting, and log management.

B. Monitoring, debugging, and reporting.

C. Logging, reporting, and debugging.

D. Alerting, monitoring, and debugging.

290. How can log data be utilized for near real-time operations?

A. By exporting logs to a local database.

B. By streaming logs to Cloud Pub/Sub.

C. By archiving logs on a physical server.

D. By deleting old logs regularly.

291. What is one of the main benefits of release management in modern software development environments?

A. It increases the time between code releases.

B. It improves the efficiency of human code reviews.

C. It enables developers to put corrected code into production quickly.

D. It eliminates the need for automated testing.

292. What is continuous deployment (CD)?

A. The practice of releasing large batches of code infrequently.

B. The practice of releasing code soon after it is completed and passes all tests.

C. The process where a human must review code before it is deployed.

D. A method of manual code deployment.

293. What is the main trade-off of continuous deployment?

A. It decreases the speed of code releases.

B. It increases the need for manual testing.

C. It introduces a higher risk of bugs due to the lack of human code review.

D. It eliminates the need for unit tests.

294. When might a team choose continuous delivery over continuous deployment?

A. When they want to release code as quickly as possible.

B. When they have highly proficient automated testing systems.

C. When they need to guarantee low risks of introducing bugs.

D. When they do not use any form of automated testing.

295. What type of test checks the smallest unit of testable code?

A. Load test

B. Acceptance test

C. Integration test

D. Unit test

296. Which type of test ensures that the code meets business requirements?

A. Unit test

B. Integration test

C. Acceptance test

D. Load test

297. What is the main purpose of integration tests?

A. To check individual functions for bugs.

B. To ensure that combined units of code work together correctly.

C. To validate that the code meets business requirements.

D. To simulate heavy workloads on the system.

298. What type of testing is useful for understanding system performance under specific conditions?
A. Unit testing
B. Integration testing
C. Acceptance testing
D. Load testing

299. Which practice involves writing comprehensive tests to detect bugs as early as possible?
A. Continuous delivery
B. Continuous deployment
C. Release management
D. Load testing

300. How can release management tools contribute to improved overall reliability?
A. By eliminating the need for automated testing.
B. By providing repositories for capturing information about releases.
C. By increasing the complexity of the release process.
D. By requiring human review for all code changes.

301. What is the primary purpose of system tests?
A. To test individual components
B. To determine the cause of failures
C. To test integrated components and the entire system's functionality
D. To introduce random failures

302. What is the initial step in system testing?
A. Performance testing

B. Regression testing
C. Sanity checks
D. Stress testing

303. What type of test ensures that previously corrected bugs are not reintroduced?
A. Performance test
B. Sanity check
C. Reliability stress test
D. Regression test

304. What is the goal of reliability stress tests?
A. To ensure system components function properly
B. To understand when and how a system will fail under heavy load
C. To introduce random failures
D. To correct bugs

305. What is chaos engineering?
A. Testing integrated system components
B. Introducing failures randomly to study their impact
C. Ensuring bugs are not reintroduced
D. Coordinating incident responses

306. What defines an incident in incident management?
A. Minor problems affecting a small group
B. Events that significantly impact a service's ability to function
C. Routine system checks
D. Regular maintenance tasks

307. What is the role of an incident commander?
A. To correct bugs

B. To coordinate the response to an incident

C. To perform sanity checks

D. To introduce random failures

308. What is the main focus during an incident management process?
A. Identifying who is responsible for the incident
B. Solving the immediate problem and restoring services
C. Conducting performance tests
D. Introducing chaos engineering tools

309. What is the purpose of a post-mortem analysis?
A. To assign blame for the incident
B. To understand why an incident happened and prevent future occurrences
C. To introduce failures randomly
D. To perform reliability stress tests

310. Why is it important that post-mortem analyses do not assign blame?
A. To ensure that bugs are not reintroduced
B. To foster an atmosphere of trust and honesty
C. To monitor components for cascading failures
D. To conduct performance tests

311. What is the primary purpose of the Analysis phase in the Software Development Lifecycle (SDLC)?
A. To write the code for the software
B. To identify the scope of the problem to be addressed
C. To test the software for bugs
D. To deploy the software

312. Which of the following is NOTNOT an advantage of buying Commercial off-the-shelf software (COTS)?
A. Faster time to solution
B. Allows developers to focus on other business requirements
C. Comes with support
D. Full control over architecture and systems design choices

313. What is often considered during the high-level design phase of the SDLC?
A. Coding of the software
B. Identifying major subcomponents of the system
C. Detailed implementation of subcomponents
D. Writing user documentation

314. In the context of SDLC, what does the term "RESTful interfaces" refer to?
A. User interface design
B. A type of messaging system
C. Interfaces used in microservice architectures
D. Interfaces for relational databases

315. Which phase of the SDLC involves mapping out in detail how the software will be structured?
A. Analysis
B. Design
C. Testing
D. Deployment

316. What is a common question to consider when evaluating options during the Analysis phase?
A. How to write the code

B. Should the organization buy a software solution or build one?

C. How to deploy the software

D. How to maintain the software

317. What is the purpose of conducting a cost-benefit analysis in the SDLC?

A. To determine the best coding language to use

B. To assess the financial cost and benefits of a project

C. To design the user interface

D. To conduct software testing

318. What does detailed design focus on in the SDLC?

A. Identifying the problem scope

B. Implementing subcomponents and defining data structures

C. Evaluating options for solving the problem

D. Deploying the software

319. Which of the following is a disadvantage of buying software?

A. Faster time to solution

B. High licensing costs

C. Comes with support

D. Allows focus on other business requirements

320. What is the potential benefit of modifying an existing application rather than building a new one from scratch?

A. Allows for complete control over design choices

B. May be the fastest option for getting a solution into production

C. Requires significant investment of time and resources

D. Allows the use of multiple coding languages

321. What is a key benefit of Continuous Integration/Continuous Development (CI/CD)?
A. Reduced need for version control
B. Faster rollout of new features to customers
C. Elimination of automated testing
D. Reduced need for user documentation

322. What type of documentation is intended for system administrators and DevOps engineers?
A. Developer documentation
B. Operations documentation
C. User documentation
D. Inline code comments

323. During the development phase of the SDLC, which types of testing are commonly performed?
A. Unit testing and integration testing
B. Performance testing and load testing
C. User acceptance testing and stress testing
D. Beta testing and alpha testing

324. Which of the following tools are often used by developers to support collaboration?
A. Integrated development environments
B. Static analysis tools
C. Version control systems
D. Code editors

325. What is the purpose of monitoring in software maintenance?
A. Collecting detailed information about the state of the system over time
B. Notifying system administrators of a condition that needs human intervention
C. Collecting data on application and infrastructure performance

D. Configuring software on servers

326. Which type of documentation should be updated frequently in an agile development environment?
A. Developer documentation
B. Operations documentation
C. User documentation
D. Configuration files

327. What is a runbook?
A. A book that contains inline comments within the code
B. A set of best practices and checklists for developers
C. Instructions on how to set up and run a service or application
D. A document outlining high-level system design details

328. Which of the following is true about the use of CI/CD in safety-critical systems?
A. CI/CD is always appropriate for safety-critical systems
B. CI/CD can replace the need for any human review in safety-critical systems
C. CI/CD may not be appropriate due to the need for rigorous validation procedures
D. CI/CD eliminates the need for automated tests in safety-critical systems

329. What is feature flagging used for in CI/CD?
A. To automate the deployment process
B. To selectively release new capabilities to customers
C. To control the level of detail saved in log messages
D. To update user documentation

330. What is the role of an architect during the early phases of the SDLC?
A. Writing unit tests

B. Performing integration testing

C. Setting standards for tools and platforms

D. Updating user documentation

331. What is the primary goal of chaos engineering?

A. To increase system performance

B. To introduce failures into a system

C. To reduce system costs

D. To enhance user experience

332. Which tool is an example of chaos engineering used by Netflix?

A. Docker Swarm

B. Kubernetes

C. Simian Army

D. Jenkins

333. What is the priority during a major incident?

A. Documenting the incident

B. Assigning blame

C. Restoring service

D. Conducting a team meeting

334. What should be the focus of an incident post-mortem review?

A. Assigning blame

B. Understanding what happened

C. Negotiating salaries

D. Planning future projects

335. What type of incident involves a disruption that affects a large portion of users or results in data loss?
A. Minor incident
B. Major incident
C. Routine maintenance
D. Security update

336. What is a key element of post-mortem culture in software development?
A. Increasing costs
B. Assigning blame
C. Learning from failures
D. Reducing testing

337. In what type of post-mortem is the effectiveness of responses to the incident assessed?
A. Project post-mortem
B. Security audit
C. Incident post-mortem
D. Performance review

338. What is one potential remediation for a misconfigured load balancer that causes application lag?
A. Adding more hardware
B. Changing the network provider
C. Developing a static code analysis script
D. Increasing user bandwidth

339. In project post-mortems, what are teams primarily looking to improve?
A. System hardware

B. Team practices

C. User interfaces

D. Marketing strategies

340. What is meant by a "blameless culture" in the context of post-mortem reviews?

A. A culture where only senior engineers are blamed

B. A culture that focuses on assigning blame to improve accountability

C. A culture where engineers feel free to disclose mistakes without fear of retribution

D. A culture that ignores all mistakes

341. What does ITIL initially stand for?

A. Information Technology Integration Library

B. Information Technology Infrastructure Library

C. Information Technology Interoperability Library

D. Information Technology Inventory Library

342. Which of the following is NOT a dimension of the ITIL model?

A. Organizations and people

B. Information and technology products

C. Financial resources and budgeting

D. Value streams and processes

343. Which group of management practices in ITIL includes architecture management?

A. General management practices

B. Service management practices

C. Technical management practices

D. Operational management practices

344. What is the primary goal of business continuity planning?
A. To enhance software development cycles
B. To maintain business operations during large-scale disruptions
C. To optimize IT service management
D. To manage financial resources efficiently

345. What does a disaster plan document typically include?
A. Marketing strategies
B. Employee performance reviews
C. Strategies for responding to a disaster
D. Financial investment plans

346. Which of the following is a component of a business impact analysis?
A. Disaster recovery testing
B. Cost estimates of different disaster scenarios
C. Employee training manuals
D. Marketing campaign performance metrics

347. What does the recovery plan describe in business continuity planning?
A. How to achieve a competitive market advantage
B. How services will be restored to normal operations
C. How to develop new software applications
D. How to allocate financial resources

348. What is the focus of disaster recovery (DR) in IT operations?
A. Enhancing user experience
B. Planning for IT service deployment in alternate environments
C. Financial auditing
D. Employee satisfaction

349. What should DR plans include to ensure proper access control replication?
A. Different roles and permissions for DR and production environments
B. A separate team for DR management
C. Procedures for replicating access controls from the normal production environment
D. Financial incentives for DR team members

350. Why is testing DR plans essential?
A. To reduce the cost of DR planning
B. To ensure the plans are effective during an actual disaster
C. To enhance marketing strategies
D. To improve software development cycles

351. What is the first stage of stakeholder management?
A. Determining roles and scope of interests
B. Identifying stakeholders
C. Developing a communications plan
D. Communicating with stakeholders

352. Which of the following stakeholders is likely to have significant influence over the release of code if it contains security vulnerabilities?
A. Marketing manager
B. Information security engineer
C. Project manager
D. Business process owner

353. What is the relationship between interest and influence in stakeholder management?
A. Interest is always higher than influence
B. Influence is always higher than interest
C. Interest describes what a stakeholder wants; influence describes their

ability to get it

D. Interest and influence are the same

354. Which of the following is NOT a form of stakeholder interest?

A. Financial interests

B. Organizational interests

C. Personnel interests

D. Geographical interests

355. In the context of stakeholder management, who is likely to have both interests and significant influence over an entire portfolio?

A. Project manager

B. Compliance officer

C. Senior vice president

D. External partner

356. What is an example of functional interests in stakeholder management?

A. A team of engineers wanting specific API functions in a new service

B. Compliance officers ensuring regulation requirements are met

C. Business owners concerned about project costs

D. HR managers assigning engineers to projects

357. Which stage of stakeholder management involves working with program and project managers to understand who else may have an interest in an initiative?

A. Identifying stakeholders

B. Determining roles and scope of interests

C. Developing a communications plan

D. Communicating with stakeholders

358. What type of initiative is focused on completing some organizational task and has a specific budget and schedule?
A. Portfolio
B. Program
C. Project
D. Strategy

359. Which of the following is a primary component of a communication plan in stakeholder management?
A. Identifying stakeholders
B. Developing project schedules
C. Communicating with and influencing stakeholders
D. Allocating project resources

360. In the context of stakeholder management, which of the following describes the scope of interests of a compliance officer?
A. Financial interests around project costs
B. Ensuring that the project meets regulation requirements around privacy and security
C. Career advancement opportunities for engineers
D. Specific API functions in a new service

361. Which of the following is an essential part of a communication plan for stakeholders?
A. Only email updates
B. Publishing updates to a project site
C. Ignoring regular updates
D. Only face-to-face meetings

362. Why is it important for architects to influence various stakeholders?
A. To ensure personal gain
B. To avoid accountability

C. To demonstrate the best architectural approaches

D. To disregard stakeholder interests

363. What is a common trait of successful digital transformation efforts?

A. Lack of communication

B. Knowledgeable leaders

C. Resistance to change

D. Ignoring workforce capabilities

364. Which methodology is discussed for managing change in the Google Cloud Professional Architect Exam?

A. Waterfall

B. Agile

C. Plan-Do-Study-Act

D. Six Sigma

365. What should be done during the 'Plan' stage of the Plan-Do-Study-Act methodology?

A. Implementing a new standard

B. Carrying out the experiment

C. Developing a change experiment and making predictions

D. Comparing results to predictions

366. What is an example of a technology-driven change for enterprises?

A. Changes in team members

B. New regulatory conditions

C. Adoption of autonomous vehicles

D. Economic factors

367. What is a key factor in ensuring the success of digital transformation?

A. Avoiding new technologies

B. Resistance to change

C. Enabling new ways of working

D. Maintaining traditional methods

368. How should results be handled in the 'Study' stage of the Plan-Do-Study-Act methodology?

A. Ignored if they don't match predictions

B. Compared to predictions and identifying learning opportunities

C. Implemented without review

D. Disregarded if negative

369. What is one example of an externally motivated change for individuals?

A. Choosing to switch teams

B. Taking a new job

C. A company reorganizing

D. Changing career paths

370. What is the purpose of a whitepaper posted by an architect?

A. To entertain stakeholders

B. To delay project implementation

C. To advocate for a particular architectural approach

D. To reduce communication with stakeholders

371. Which of the following is NOT a responsibility of an architect in terms of team skill development?

A. Defining skills needed to execute programs and projects

B. Providing direct customer support for service issues

C. Identifying skill gaps on a team or in an organization

D. Mentoring engineers and other professionals

372. What is the primary goal of customer success management?
A. Increasing the number of products sold
B. Enhancing the company's marketing strategy
C. Helping customers derive value from the products and services provided
D. Reducing the cost of customer acquisition

373. In customer success management, which stage involves engaging new customers?
A. Professional services
B. Customer acquisition
C. Training and support
D. Marketing and sales

374. Which of the following activities is least likely to involve an architect directly?
A. Cost estimating
B. Customer acquisition
C. Professional services
D. Cost budgeting

375. What is the first step in cost management?
A. Cost estimating
B. Cost budgeting
C. Resource planning
D. Cost control

376. Which of the following is NOT a type of cost considered in cost estimating?
A. Human resources costs
B. Marketing costs

C. Infrastructure costs

D. Capital costs

377. Which stage of cost management involves making decisions about how to allocate funds?

A. Resource planning

B. Cost estimating

C. Cost budgeting

D. Cost control

378. Which of the following stages of customer success management involves consulting services?

A. Customer acquisition

B. Marketing and sales

C. Professional services

D. Training and support

379. What type of planning requires identifying projects and programs that need funding and prioritizing their needs?

A. Cost control

B. Resource planning

C. Cost budgeting

D. Cost estimating

380. Which of the following is NOT a part of the four basic stages of customer success management?

A. Customer acquisition

B. Cost control

C. Professional services

D. Training and support

381. What is the standard HTTP return code for a successful API call?
A. 200
B. 400
C. 401
D. 404

382. Which of the following HTTP error codes indicates that a request contained an invalid argument?
A. 500
B. 403
C. 400
D. 503

383. What is the purpose of an API key?
A. To encrypt data in transit
B. To uniquely identify a user of a service
C. To limit resource consumption
D. To specify the API version number

384. Which part of a JWT contains claims about the issuer, subject, or token?
A. Header
B. Payload
C. Signature
D. None of the above

385. Which of the following is a method of resource limiting in APIs?
A. Data-driven testing
B. Rate limiting
C. Keyword-driven testing
D. Model-based testing

386. In the context of API security, what does HTTPS provide?
A. Authentication
B. Rate limiting
C. Encryption for data in transit
D. Authorization

387. Which of the following testing frameworks uses structured data sets to drive testing?
A. Modularity-driven testing
B. Keyword-driven testing
C. Data-driven testing
D. Model-based testing

388. In JWT, what is the purpose of the signature?
A. To specify the type of token
B. To contain claims about the token
C. To secure the token using a secret
D. To encrypt the payload

389. What is a common use of predefined roles in IAM on the Google Cloud Platform?
A. To limit API call rates
B. To track usage by user
C. To accommodate common requirements for different types of users
D. To define API versions

390. Which HTTP error code indicates that the requested resource was not found?
A. 500
B. 404

C. 401

D. 403

391. During which phase of the migration process should you take inventory of applications and infrastructure?

A. Optimization

B. Assessment

C. Data Migration

D. Application Migration

392. What is the primary goal during the pilot phase of a cloud migration?

A. To optimize cloud implementation

B. To migrate all data to the cloud

C. To migrate one or two applications and gain experience

D. To assess compliance and licensing issues

393. What should be considered for applications that require high availability during the migration process?

A. Licensing issues

B. Recovery time objectives and failover databases

C. Application documentation

D. Manual operations for normal operations

394. Which migration phase focuses on moving applications to the cloud after data has been migrated?

A. Data Migration

B. Pilot

C. Application Migration

D. Optimization

395. What is a critical task during the optimization phase of a cloud migration?

A. Developing experience running applications in the cloud

B. Migrating data using gsutil or Google Cloud Transfer Appliance

C. Adding Cloud Operations monitoring and logging to applications

D. Assessing compliance and licensing issues

396. Why might some applications be deemed unsuitable for cloud migration?

A. They are developed by a third-party

B. They are batch-processing jobs

C. They have minimal in-house expertise

D. They are scheduled to be removed from service soon

397. During which phase would you synchronize on-premises data with cloud data?

A. Assessment

B. Pilot

C. Data Migration

D. Optimization

398. Which tool can replace third-party ETL tools during the optimization phase?

A. gsutil

B. Google Cloud Transfer Appliance

C. Cloud Dataflow

D. Kubernetes

399. What should you document about an application to understand its migration risk?

A. The number of users

B. The production level and service-level agreements (SLAs)

C. The type of cloud service to be used

D. The cost of the current infrastructure

400. What is a key consideration for applications that must be available 24/7?

A. Compliance issues

B. Licensing costs

C. Tier 1 categorization

D. Manual operations for maintenance

401. What is the primary consideration when determining if an on-premises software license can be used in the cloud?

A. The vendor's hardware requirements

B. The vendor's licensing restrictions

C. The vendor's support policies

D. The cost of the license

402. What should you consider if you have a single site license for an on-premises application but plan to run it in multiple regions in the cloud?

A. The compatibility of the software with the cloud provider

B. The cost of cloud storage

C. The suitability of the single site license for multi-region use

D. The availability of customer support

403. Which of the following is NOT a component of a Virtual Private Cloud (VPC) in Google Cloud?

A. Networks

B. VPNs

C. Subnets

D. Firewalls

404. When planning for network scalability, which service can be used to distribute traffic globally using a single anycast IP address?
A. Cloud Interconnect
B. Cloud Load Balancing
C. Cloud DNS
D. Cloud CDN

405. What is the primary role of Cloud VPN in a GCP network?
A. To manage DNS records
B. To load balance traffic globally
C. To link your Google Cloud VPC to an on-premises network
D. To distribute static content globally

406. Which IAM role would you assign to someone who needs full permissions to manage network resources?
A. Network Viewer
B. Security Admin
C. Compute Instance Admin
D. Network Admin

407. Which type of load balancing is suitable for dealing with spikes in TCP and IP traffic?
A. HTTP(S) layer 7 load balancing
B. Network load balancing
C. Application load balancing
D. Content load balancing

408. What should you use if you need a consistent long-term IP address for a public website or API endpoint?
A. Ephemeral IP address

B. Dynamic IP address
C. Static IP address
D. Private IP address

409. Which service provides direct access to Google's edge network?
A. Carrier peering
B. Direct peering
C. CDN interconnect
D. IPsec tunnel

410. What is the importance of custom routes in a VPC?
A. They are necessary for VPN connections.
B. They help implement many-to-one NAT or transparent proxies.
C. They automatically manage subnets.
D. They provide DNS services.

411. What term did Ward Cunningham coined to describe the process of making reasonable choices to meet an objective, like releasing code by a particular date?
A. Financial Debt
B. Technical Debt
C. Architectural Debt
D. Interest Debt

412. Which of the following is NOT a reason for incurring technical debt?
A. Insufficient understanding of requirements
B. Overstaffing a project
C. Need to deliver some functional code by a set time or within a fixed budget
D. Lack of coding standards

413. What is the ideal way to address technical debt?

A. Ignoring it

B. Adding more features

C. Refactoring code and implementing better solutions

D. Hiring more developers

414. What type of technical debt is incurred when a reasonable architecture design choice requires rework later?

A. Code technical debt

B. Architectural design debt

C. Environment debt

D. Financial debt

415. Which of the following is an example of environment debt?

A. Poor error handling in code

B. Designing an application for vertical scaling

C. Implementing a data partitioning scheme

D. Building applications and running tests manually instead of using a CI/CD platform

416. What should be one of the first actions taken in the next phase of a project after incurring technical debt to meet a deadline?

A. Add new features

B. Revise the code to improve error handling and perform thorough code reviews

C. Hire new developers

D. Increase the project budget

417. Which standard method uses HTTP POST to create an object in a REST API?

A. List
B. Get
C. Create
D. Update

418. What kind of resources consist of a single entity in an API?
A. Collections
B. Simple resources
C. Custom methods
D. Complex resources

419. Which HTTP method is used by the 'Delete' operation in a REST API?
A. GET
B. POST
C. PUT
D. DELETE

420. What is a potential consequence of not paying down technical debt?
A. Increased project funding
B. Enhanced application reliability
C. Problems in production that adversely impact users
D. Faster development times

421. What is defined as a sequence of steps to execute in the context of testing?
A. A test
B. A simulation
C. A migration
D. A rebuild

422. Where is the data for each test typically stored?
A. In the application code
B. In a spreadsheet or another document
C. In the cloud
D. In the database schema

423. Which testing framework uses a simulation program to generate test data?
A. Keyword test frameworks
B. Model-based testing
C. Test-driven development
D. Hybrid testing

424. What is the key characteristic of test-driven development?
A. It uses a graphical user interface
B. It incorporates testing into the development process
C. It relies on manual testing
D. It involves migration to the cloud

425. Which of the following is a Python testing framework?
A. Selenium
B. JUnit
C. pytest
D. Katalon Studio

426. Which tool is widely used for browser automation?
A. JUnit
B. Selenium
C. pytest
D. Katalon Studio

427. What type of migration involves moving infrastructure and data with minimal changes?
A. Rebuild in the cloud
B. Lift and shift
C. Move and improve
D. Hybrid migration

428. What should be performed when implementing a lift-and-shift migration?
A. Develop new application code
B. Perform an inventory of all applications, data sources, and infrastructure
C. Create a new database schema
D. Automate all testing

429. What is Katalon Studio built on?
A. pytest
B. JUnit
C. Selenium
D. Kubernetes Engine

430. Which testing framework encourages developing small amounts of code and frequent testing?
A. Keyword test frameworks
B. Model-based testing
C. Test-driven development
D. Hybrid testing

431. What is the recommended way to transfer data from AWS S3 to Google Cloud?
A. gsutil command-line utility
B. Google Transfer Appliance

C. Google Transfer Service

D. Third-party vendors

432. Which tool is most suitable for transferring data from on-premises to Google Cloud?

A. Google Transfer Appliance

B. gsutil command-line utility

C. Google Transfer Service

D. Third-party vendors

433. What is one advantage of using the gsutil command-line utility?

A. It can only transfer small files

B. It does not support parallel loading

C. It supports restarts after failures

D. It cannot be tuned with command-line parameters

434. Which factor does NOT directly affect the time required to transfer data?

A. Volume of data

B. Network bandwidth

C. Time of day

D. Location of data

435. What is the capacity of the largest Google Transfer Appliance currently available?

A. 50 TB

B. 100 TB

C. 480 TB

D. 1 PB

436. Which GCP SDK component is used for managing Kubernetes clusters?
A. gcloud
B. gsutil
C. bq
D. kubectl

437. Which of the following is NOT a default component installed with the GCP SDK?
A. gcloud
B. gsutil
C. bq
D. cbt

438. Which command is used to enable user account authorization in the GCP SDK?
A. gcloud init
B. gcloud auth activate-service-account
C. gcloud components install
D. gcloud config set account

439. What should be considered when deciding how to transfer large volumes of data to Google Cloud?
A. The color of the cables
B. Time constraints on data transfer
C. The brand of the network router
D. The number of employees

440. What is the function of the bq command-line tool in the GCP SDK?
A. Interacting with most GCP services
B. Working with BigQuery

C. Managing Kubernetes clusters

D. Working with Cloud Storage

441. What is a recommended method to transfer less than 10 TB of data from an on-premises data center to Google Cloud Storage?

A. Google Transfer Appliance

B. gsutil

C. USB Drive

D. FTP

442. If no downtime is acceptable during a system switchover, what is a recommended approach?

A. Schedule the switchover during off-peak hours

B. Run on-premises and cloud systems in parallel before switching over

C. Notify users about the system being unavailable

D. Perform the switchover immediately

443. What should you investigate and consider when planning a data migration with data governance requirements?

A. Data encryption methods

B. Data governance policies and regulations

C. Data replication techniques

D. Data format conversion

444. Which Google Cloud service is recommended for monitoring the performance of a migrated system?

A. Cloud Build

B. Cloud Operations Logging

C. Google Transfer Appliance

D. gsutil

445. What is the preferred migration method for relational databases if an export-based migration is not feasible?
A. Create a replica database in the Google Cloud
B. Use flat file transfer
C. Perform a direct database copy
D. Use a third-party data migration service

446. Which factor is NOT mentioned as critical in planning data migration?
A. Network bandwidth
B. Time and cost
C. Data encryption
D. Order of data transfer

447. Which service could be used if you need to automate deployment in the cloud?
A. Cloud Build
B. FTP
C. Google Transfer Appliance
D. DNS

448. What is a consideration for determining the method to transfer large data volumes (over 20 TB) to the cloud?
A. Use of portable hard drives
B. Google Transfer Appliance
C. Manual data entry
D. Email attachments

449. What should be done to ensure a consistent export of a relational database during migration?
A. Lock the database for read operations

B. Lock the database for write operations
C. Perform the export during peak hours
D. Use manual export techniques

450. What is the best approach if the data volume is between 10 TB and 20 TB and network bandwidth is limited?
A. Google Transfer Appliance
B. gsutil
C. USB Drive
D. Email attachments

Answers

1. Answer: B

Explanation: The planning phase should start with collecting business requirements, as they define the operational landscape in which the solution will be developed. These requirements often impact costs, customer experience, and operational improvements.

2. Answer: B

Explanation: Managed services reduce the workload on systems administrators and DevOps engineers by eliminating some of the manual work required to manage platforms, such as backups and patching.

3. Answer: C

Explanation: Preemptible VMs are low-cost instances that can run up to 24 hours before being preempted. They are suitable for batch processing and other easily recoverable tasks.

4. Answer: C

Explanation: Autoscaling adjusts the number of instances based on demand, increasing during high demand and decreasing during low demand, which helps optimize infrastructure costs.

5. Answer: C

Explanation: Business requirements are complex because they span various functions and needs. To fully satisfy them, a combination of technical

Answers

VERSAtile Reads

solutions is often necessary. These solutions must integrate well to handle diverse needs, ensure security and compliance, optimize performance, enhance user experience, manage data effectively, automate processes, and allow for customization. This multifaceted approach ensures that all aspects of the business operate efficiently and can adapt to changing demands.

6. Answer: B

Explanation: Agile software development practices are designed to support rapid development, testing, deployment, and feedback, enabling constant innovation.

7. Answer: B

Explanation: CI/CD practices involve integrating small amounts of new code frequently, which allows for easier review, debugging, and quicker feedback from colleagues and customers.

8. Answer: B

Explanation: Lift-and-shift migration is considered when a business needs to move to the cloud quickly to avoid large capital expenditures or long-term leases in data centers.

9. Answer: A

Explanation: It's important to assess if the monolithic application depends on deprecated components, as this will impact whether it can be migrated with minimal modifications.

10. Answer: C

Explanation: A finance department may only need access to accounting systems during business hours, allowing upgrades and maintenance to occur during off-hours without impacting availability.

11. Answer: C

Explanation: SLOs are defined in terms of specific performance metrics like availability, durability, or response times to ensure that a service meets certain standards.

12. Answer: C

Explanation: Cloud Operations logging is used to collect information about significant events like a disk running out of space, which helps in monitoring compliance with SLOs.

13. Answer: C

Explanation: HIPAA is a healthcare regulation focused on protecting the privacy and security of healthcare information.

14. Answer: C

Explanation: Operational expenditures are the day-to-day expenses required to run a business, as opposed to capital expenditures, which are for long-term investments.

15. Answer: B

Explanation: KPIs are metrics that provide information on how well an organization is achieving its important objectives.

16. Answer: B

Explanation: Collecting and making metrics and log events available can help engineers quickly diagnose and resolve issues, reducing recovery time.

17. Answer: B

Explanation: SOX, short for the Sarbanes-Oxley Act of 2002, is a comprehensive regulation enacted in response to accounting scandals like Enron and WorldCom. It aims to enhance corporate governance, financial transparency, and the accuracy of financial reporting in public companies. The act mandates strict internal controls, financial disclosures, and independent audits to prevent fraudulent practices and protect investors' interests.

18. Answer: C

Explanation: Digital transformation involves adopting new technologies to develop new products, improve customer service, and optimize operations.

19. Answer: C

Explanation: Brick-and-mortar businesses refer to companies with physical locations where they conduct their operations.

20. Answer: C

Explanation: Governance involves the procedures and practices used to ensure that organizational policies and principles are followed correctly.

21. **Answer: C**

Explanation: Compute Engine is the best option for running a virtual machine with a specific hardened version of Linux because it provides the most control over the operating system and environment configurations.

22. **Answer: C**

Explanation: Spanner offers global, strongly consistent transactional data storage, making it the correct choice for applications requiring these features.

23. **Answer: C**

Explanation: Coldline storage is designed for data accessed no more than once a year, making it suitable for long-term archival storage.

24. **Answer: C**

Explanation: Dedicated Interconnect is used when the bandwidth requirements are 10 Gbps or greater, providing a direct physical connection between the on-premises data center and Google Cloud Platform.

25. **Answer: B**

Explanation: Cloud Datastore is a good option for a document store requiring a flexible schema, offering NoSQL capabilities for such use cases.

26. **Answer: B**

Explanation: Latency is a metric that reflects how well a service-level objective is being met, making it an example of an SLI.

27. Answer: D

Explanation: Bigtable is well-suited for ingesting large volumes of time-series data at low latency, making it the best option for this requirement.

28. Answer: D

Explanation: Autoscalers and instance groups help ensure scalability by adapting infrastructure to the load on the system, adding or removing resources as needed.

29. Answer: B

Explanation: Cloud SQL is a good choice for a regional-scale relational database, offering a managed service for SQL databases.

30. Answer: B

Explanation: Firewalls and firewall rules are essential for structuring virtual private clouds (VPCs) and managing the types of traffic allowed in or out of the network.

31. Answer: B

Explanation: Dress4Win's infrastructure is insufficient for the application's rapid growth, driving the need for a full migration to a public cloud.

32. Answer: C

Explanation: Dress4Win's technical environment includes MySQL databases, Redis servers, and Apache Hadoop/Spark servers, but not Microsoft SQL Server databases.

33. Answer: B

Explanation: One of the key business requirements for Dress4Win's cloud migration is to improve business agility and speed of innovation through rapidly provisioning new resources.

34. Answer: B

Explanation: Supporting the failover of the production environment to the cloud during an emergency is a crucial technical requirement.

35. Answer: B

Explanation: Investors are concerned about Dress4Win's ability to scale and contain costs with the current infrastructure.

36. Answer: B

Explanation: The statement that traffic patterns are highest in the mornings and weekend evenings, with 80% of capacity sitting idle at other times, indicates an opportunity for using autoscaling.

37. Answer: C

Explanation: Dress4Win uses a NAS appliance for centralized storage of images, logs, and backups. This setup ensures easy access, efficient management, and reliable backups for their operational needs.

38. Answer: C

Explanation: Dress4Win uses Apache Hadoop/Spark servers for data analysis and real-time trending calculations.

39. Answer: B

Explanation: RabbitMQ servers at Dress4Win serve the critical functions of messaging, managing social notifications, and handling events efficiently. This setup ensures reliable communication and real-time updates across their applications and services.

40. Answer: B

Explanation: Improving security by defining and adhering to a set of security and IAM best practices is a key business requirement for Dress4Win's cloud migration.

41. Answer: B

Explanation: An architect's responsibility in systems integration is to ensure that systems work together, even though business requirements will not specify technical details about how applications should function together.

42. Answer: B

Explanation: The case study suggests using analytic platforms such as Cloud Dataproc or BigQuery for processing customer data to generate recommended matches.

43. Answer. B

Explanation: Mountkirk Games likely uses a microservices architecture, where single services implement specific functions of an application accessible through APIs.

44. Answer: C

Explanation: Cloud Endpoints are recommended to manage APIs and help secure and monitor calls to microservices, ensuring proper authentication and security controls.

45. Answer: B

Explanation: Cloud Pub/Sub is suggested for handling data ingestion from vehicles in real-time. It allows decoupling and buffering, ensuring data is not lost if ingestion services cannot keep up.

46. Answer: B

Explanation: Architects should gather details on what features of the data are significant to dealers and how dealers would access the data to support better product positioning.

47. Answer: C

Explanation: Nearline storage is appropriate for data accessed once per month or less, offering cost savings for infrequent access.

48. Answer: B

Explanation: Architects need to consider the expected volume of data to plan for adequate storage capacity and accurately estimate storage costs.

49. Answer: C

Explanation: Archiving large volumes of data can benefit machine learning models, making it advisable to archive data for potential future use.

50. Answer: B

Explanation: Procedures for data retention and deletion need to be developed to manage the data lifecycle effectively, either archiving or deleting data as per business requirements.

51. Answer: B

Explanation: Mechanical engineering and manufacturing processes are outside the scope of cloud solution design, which focuses more on analytical skills, data management, and predictive modeling.

52. Answer: B

Explanation: Releasing incremental improvements aligns with agile software development and continuous integration/continuous deployment practices.

53. Answer: B

Explanation: Cloud Operations is mentioned as a tool for collecting metrics and logging to help identify problems, bottlenecks, and other issues in the solution.

54. Answer: A

Explanation: BigQuery is recommended as a data warehouse solution for storing large amounts of data for use in data analysis.

55. Answer: A

Explanation: Cloud SQL is a managed relational database service providing MySQL and PostgreSQL databases on the Google Cloud Platform.

56. Answer: C

Explanation: Total cost of ownership (TCO) includes all expenses related to maintaining a service, such as software licensing, cloud computing costs, and network connectivity charges.

57. Answer: D

Explanation: Increasing the number of on-premises servers does not reduce costs in the context of cloud-based solutions. Managed services, preemptible virtual machines, and data lifecycle management are mentioned as ways to reduce costs.

58. Answer: B

Explanation: Analytical skills are needed to better understand customer needs and equipment performance, which fall within the scope of cloud solution design.

59. Answer: A

Explanation: After finding a feasible technical solution, it is generally a good practice to start optimizing that solution for costs without trying to minimize the cost of each component separately.

60. **Answer: B**

Explanation: Managed services are a good option when they provide functionality that is difficult or expensive to implement, such as developing a machine vision application.

61. **Answer: C**

Explanation: Cloud Speech-to-Text is indeed a service offered by Google Cloud Platform (GCP) that allows developers to convert spoken language into text. It utilizes advanced machine learning models to recognize over 120 languages and variants, supporting real-time speech recognition and transcription. This service is useful for applications ranging from voice commands in mobile devices to transcription of audio content in customer service interactions and more.

62. **Answer: B**

Explanation: Memorystore is a Google Cloud service for caching frequently accessed data to reduce latency in applications. It supports Redis and Memcached, providing managed infrastructure to handle scaling and maintenance, allowing developers to focus on optimizing application performance.

63. **Answer: B**

Explanation: Preemptible VMs are not suitable for applications that require high availability because Google can shut them down at any time and will be shut down after running for 24 hours.

64. Answer: C

Explanation: AutoML Tables is the Google Cloud Platform managed service designed for creating machine learning models specifically for structured data.

65. Answer: A

Explanation: Cloud Data Fusion is Google Cloud Platform's data integration and ETL (Extract, Transform, Load) tool, designed to simplify the process of building and managing data pipelines.

66. Answer: B

Explanation: Cloud Storage's lifecycle management can delete an object or change its storage class based on specific conditions.

67. Answer: D

Explanation: Coldline storage is a cost-effective Google Cloud Storage solution designed for infrequently accessed data, ideal for long-term storage and archival purposes. It offers lower costs compared to more frequently accessed storage options like Nearline or Standard, making it suitable for data that is accessed no more than once a year.

68. Answer: B

Explanation: Cloud Memorystore is a fully managed service provided by Google Cloud Platform that utilizes Redis, an open-source, in-memory data structure store, to cache and serve frequently accessed data. It helps reduce latency and improves application responsiveness by storing data in-memory, making it readily available for quick retrieval.

69. **Answer: B**

Explanation: Cloud Datalab is an interactive data analysis and exploration tool offered by Google Cloud Platform. It is based on Jupyter Notebooks, providing a collaborative environment where users can write and execute Python code, visualize data, and share insights.

70. **Answer: B**

Explanation: Cloud Spanner is a globally distributed relational database service offered by Google Cloud Platform. It combines the benefits of traditional relational databases, such as strong consistency and SQL support, with horizontal scalability and global distribution to support large-scale applications with high availability and low latency.

71. **Answer: B**

Explanation: The distance between the location of stored data and where it is processed is an important consideration as it affects both the time it takes to read and write the data as well as network costs for transmitting the data.

72. **Answer: A**

Explanation: In stream processing, it is common to assume that no data older than a specified time will arrive, and processes may wait for a certain period before assuming the data will never arrive.

73. Answer: B

Explanation: The Health Insurance Portability and Accountability Act (HIPAA) addresses the privacy and security of medical information in the United States.

74. Answer: B

Explanation: Access controls are a primary tool for protecting data integrity, ensuring that only authorized persons or service accounts can modify data.

75. Answer: D

Explanation: When transitioning from batch to stream processing, it is essential to consider how to handle late arriving and missing data to ensure the processing is accurate and timely.

76. Answer: C

Explanation: The Payment Card Industry Data Security Standard (PCI DSS) specifies security controls that must be in place to protect cardholders' data.

77. Answer: A

Explanation: Encrypting data both at rest and in motion is a common practice to protect data throughout its lifecycle.

78. Answer: C

Explanation: Defense in depth is a principle that assumes any security control may be compromised, and therefore systems should be protected with multiple different types of controls.

79. Answer: A

Explanation: ROI stands for Return on Investment and is expressed as a percentage. It measures the monetary value of an investment by comparing the value after the investment to its cost.

80. Answer: B

Explanation: A KPI, or Key Performance Indicator, is a measurable value that indicates how well an organization is achieving its objectives, and it is important for measuring the success of a cloud project.

81. Answer: C

Explanation: A service level agreement (SLA) of 99.99% availability translates to allowing up to 8.64 seconds of downtime per day. This level of availability is often required for critical systems and services where minimal disruption is essential for operations.

82. Answer: B

Explanation: Using a single server increases the risk of downtime; redundancy through multiple servers is preferred.

83. Answer: C

Explanation: A managed instance group in Google Compute Engine is used to maintain multiple virtual machines (VMs) that share the same configuration. This means that each VM in the group is created from the same instance template, ensuring consistency across all VMs. Managed instance groups are beneficial for scaling applications because they allow you to easily add or remove instances based on load, and they help maintain high availability by automatically managing the distribution and lifecycle of VMs in the group.

84. Answer: B

Explanation: Live migration is a feature that moves virtual machines between physical servers without causing downtime, ensuring continuous operation during maintenance or hardware failures

85. Answer: B

Explanation: Global load balancing distributes workload across multiple regions, enhancing availability and reducing latency

86. Answer: C

Explanation Pods are the smallest unit of deployment in Kubernetes, usually containing one or more tightly coupled containers

87. Answer: B

Explanation: Auto-healing automatically detects application failures and replaces the failing instances with new ones to maintain system reliability and availability.

88. Answer: C

Explanation: App Engine is a fully managed compute service where users are not responsible for maintaining the availability of computing resources

89. Answer: C

Explanation: Regional clusters distribute VMs across multiple zones, enhancing availability and fault tolerance

90. Answer: A

Explanation: A 99.999% availability SLA (Service Level Agreement) allows for 26.3 seconds of monthly downtime. This level of availability is often referred to as "five nines," indicating a very high standard of reliability where downtime is minimized to just seconds per month on average.

91. Answer: C

Explanation: BigQuery is a fully managed database with load distribution and autoscaling, which allows it to scale dynamically based on game activity.

92. Answer: C

Explanation: Regional replication in Bigtable involves replicating data across multiple zones within the same region. This approach enhances availability by ensuring that data remains accessible even if one zone or a portion of the infrastructure experiences issues. It also helps in achieving higher durability and reliability of data stored in Bigtable, which is crucial for applications requiring low-latency access and high availability.

93. Answer: B

Explanation: The Premium Network Tier uses Google's internal network designed for high availability and low latency, making it ideal for global network availability concerns.

94. Answer: B

Explanation: Bigtable is an optimal solution for real-time applications that require writing large volumes of time-series data with low latency. Its scalability, low-latency reads and writes, columnar storage, and regional replication ensure efficient handling and availability of time-series data.

95. Answer: B

Explanation: Redundant network connections ensure that the network remains available even if one connection fails.

96. Answer: C

Explanation: Cloud Storage offers highly available storage solutions that are particularly suitable for storing a variety of data types, including images, logs, and backups. It provides durability, scalability, and accessibility across different regions, making it an ideal choice for applications that require reliable storage capabilities.

97. Answer: B

Explanation: Regional persistent disks in Google Cloud Platform provide higher availability by replicating data synchronously across multiple zones within a region. This replication ensures that data remains accessible even if one zone within the region experiences an outage or maintenance event. This feature enhances the reliability and availability of storage for applications that require redundancy and fault tolerance.

98. Answer: C

Explanation: Cloud Operations Monitoring is a Google Cloud service that monitors application performance and infrastructure health in real-time, offering customizable alerts and detailed metrics to ensure reliable and efficient operations.

99. Answer: C

Explanation: Redundant network connections ensure higher network availability by providing alternative paths for data transmission.

100. Answer: B

Explanation: Stateful applications inherently maintain state information, which is difficult to distribute across multiple instances. This complicates horizontal scaling, making it challenging to manage state consistency and synchronization.

101. Answer: C

Explanation: Cloud Functions is a serverless computing service provided by cloud providers like Google Cloud, AWS (Lambda), and Azure (Functions). It allows you to run small, single-purpose functions in response to events without managing infrastructure. Key features include automatic scaling, cost efficiency, and integration with other cloud services. Common use cases include data processing, file handling, API backends, IoT, and task automation.

102. Answer: C

Explanation: Standard instances offer balanced CPU and memory. Highmem instances provide more memory, suitable for memory-intensive tasks, while high CPU instances offer more CPUs, ideal for compute-intensive workloads.

103. Answer: B

Explanation: Google Kubernetes Engine (GKE) is a managed Kubernetes service provided by Google Cloud Platform for deploying, managing, and scaling containerized applications.

104. Answer: C

Explanation: Preemptible VMs are cost-effective instances on the Google Cloud Platform designed for short-term use. They can run for a maximum of 24 hours and might be terminated by GCP at any time, making them ideal for fault-tolerant workloads and batch jobs.

105. Answer: A

Explanation: Secure Boot is a security feature that ensures that only trusted and authenticated software is loaded during the boot process. It uses UEFI firmware to verify the digital signatures of all boot components, preventing unauthorized or malicious software from running.

106. Answer: C

Explanation: A service account is used to grant permissions to VMs, allowing them to perform actions on Google Cloud services without user intervention. It authenticates the VM or application, enabling secure and automated access to resources.

107. **Answer: D**

Explanation: When creating a VM boot image, you can choose between Local SSD, Standard Persistent Disk, or SSD Persistent Disk. Local SSDs offer high performance but are non-persistent. Standard Persistent Disks provide reliable, durable storage. SSD Persistent Disks offer faster performance with lower latency, ideal for I/O-intensive applications. Choose based on your application's performance and persistence needs.

108. **Answers: C**

Explanation: Sole tenancy enables running VMs on dedicated physical servers that exclusively host VMs from the same project. This setup ensures strict isolation and compliance with specific regulatory or security requirements.

109. **Answer: A**

Explanation: Managed instance groups contain identically configured VMs specified by an instance template, whereas unmanaged instance groups do not require VMs to be identical and are used for preexisting cluster configurations.

110. **Answer: C**

Explanation: All boot images in the Google Cloud Platform are encrypted automatically. You can choose between predefined boot images, custom boot images based on predefined ones, and specify persistent disk types, but you cannot opt for boot images without encryption.

111. Answer: D

Explanation: The first-generation App Engine Standard supports Python 2.7, Java 8, PHP 5.5, and Go 1.9. Python 3.7 is supported in the second-generation App Engine Standard.

112. Answer: C

Explanation: Python 2.7, PHP 5.5, and Go 1.9 in the first-generation App Engine Standard can access the network only through a URL Fetch API.

113. Answer: A

Explanation: App Engine Standard is ideal for applications requiring quick scaling in response to traffic fluctuations. It automatically adjusts the number of instances based on demand, ensuring efficient handling of varying loads. For instance, with startup times of just a few seconds, it provides a responsive and scalable environment, making it suitable for applications with unpredictable or rapidly changing traffic patterns.

114. Answer: B

Explanation: App Engine Flexible has an instance startup time on the order of minutes, making it suitable for applications that can tolerate slightly longer startup times but require more customization and flexibility in terms of runtime and system configurations.

115. Answer: B

Explanation: Cloud Pub/Sub is an excellent option for a publish/subscribe-type messaging service, providing reliable, scalable, and asynchronous communication between independent applications.

116. Answer: D

Explanation: By default, App Engine Flexible supports Java 8, Python 2.7 and Python 3.6, Node.js, Ruby, PHP, .NET core, and Go. Java 11 is not mentioned as a default supported runtime.

117. Answer: B

Explanation: In-App Engine Flexible, containers are restarted at least once per week to ensure the underlying infrastructure remains updated and secure. This regular restart helps maintain the health and performance of the application.

118. Answer: C

Explanation: The scheduler in Kubernetes is responsible for determining which nodes to run pods. It makes these decisions based on factors like resource requirements, policies, and current cluster state to optimize workload distribution.

119. Answer: C

Explanation: A complete deployment, often referred to as a "big bang" deployment, updates all instances of the application simultaneously. The primary disadvantage of this approach is that if there are any issues or bugs in the new code, they will affect all users at the same time, potentially leading to widespread problems and disruptions. This can be particularly problematic because it makes rollback and troubleshooting more challenging, as all users are experiencing the same issues at once.

120. Answer: B

Explanation: A service is an abstraction in Kubernetes with a stable API endpoint and stable IP address, allowing applications to communicate reliably with pods.

121. **Answer: D**

Explanation: An Ingress is an object that controls external access to services running in a Kubernetes cluster. An Ingress Controller must be running in a cluster for an Ingress to function.

122. **Answer: B**

Explanation: A PersistentVolumeClaim (PVC) is a logical way to request and link a pod to persistent storage in Kubernetes. It allows pods to access persistent volumes (PVs), which represent the actual storage resources allocated for use by the pods. PVCs abstract the storage details and enable dynamic provisioning of storage resources.

123. **Answer: C**

Explanation: Cloud Functions on Google Cloud Platform is a serverless compute service that enables developers to deploy and run event-driven functions without managing servers. It supports multiple programming languages like Node.js, Python, Go, Java, and .NET, allowing developers to respond dynamically to events such as HTTP requests, database changes, and messaging events. Cloud Functions scales automatically, charges only for the compute time used, and abstract infrastructure complexities, making it ideal for cost-effectively building agile and scalable applications.

124. **Answer: A**

Explanation: Cloud Functions can respond to HTTP events with actions such as GET, POST, PUT, DELETE, and OPTIONS, among other events like Cloud Storage and Cloud Pub/Sub events.

125. Answer: B

Explanation: StatefulSets are used to manage pods with the state by assigning unique identifiers to them, ensuring that they are not functionally interchangeable.

126. Answer: B

Explanation: Python 3, Go, Node.js 8 and 10. Cloud Functions, particularly on Google Cloud, support these specific programming languages for writing serverless functions. Python 3 is known for its readability and simplicity, making it a popular choice among developers. Go, designed at Google, is appreciated for its efficiency and performance. Node.js (versions 8 and 10) is widely used for building scalable network applications due to its asynchronous, event-driven nature.

127. Answer: C

Explanation: A ReplicaSet in Kubernetes is responsible for ensuring a specified number of identical pod replicas are running concurrently within the cluster. It continuously monitors the state of the pods. It takes actions to maintain the desired number of replicas, scaling them up or down as needed based on the defined configuration and current cluster conditions. ReplicaSets are crucial for maintaining application availability, scalability, and resilience by automatically managing pod instances to match the desired replica count.

128. Answer: B

VERSAtile Reads

Explanation: Deployment Manager is used to specify infrastructure as code, allowing teams to reproduce environments rapidly and apply software engineering practices like code reviews and version control.

129. Answer: C

Explanation: Cloud Functions are used for event-driven processing, such as executing code in response to a file being uploaded to Cloud Storage.

130. Answer: C

Explanation: Google Kubernetes Engine (GKE) provides a platform for deploying, managing, and scaling containerized services. Kubernetes is an open-source system for automating the deployment, scaling, and management of containerized applications, and GKE is Google Cloud's managed Kubernetes service.

131. Answer: B

Explanation: Assigning sensors based on machine ID can skew workload distribution because some machines may have significantly more sensors than others, leading to an imbalanced load across servers.

132. Answer: C

Explanation: Separating state data from volatile instances allows the system to maintain the state information even if an instance fails.

133. Answer: C

Explanation: Cloud Memorystore is a managed Redis service on the Google Cloud Platform, offering low-latency access to data. It's optimized for caching and storing transient state information, providing high performance and scalability. GCP handles infrastructure management, ensuring reliability and allowing seamless integration with Redis applications through standard protocols. This makes it ideal for applications requiring fast data retrieval and real-time processing capabilities.

134. Answer: C

Explanation: Databases are complex applications that often demand substantial effort to maintain and optimize. They store and manage structured data, serving as critical components in most software systems. Tasks such as ensuring data integrity, optimizing queries for performance, and scaling to handle increasing loads can be challenging and time-consuming. Database administrators and developers invest significant resources in monitoring, tuning, and securing databases to ensure they operate efficiently and reliably. Advances in cloud services have simplified some aspects of database management, offering managed solutions that alleviate operational burdens while still requiring attention to performance and scalability.

135. Answer: B

Explanation: Asynchronous operations enable workflows to proceed without waiting for lengthy tasks to finish, thereby minimizing delays and improving overall efficiency.

136. Answer: D

Explanation: Cloud Pub/Sub is an efficient messaging service designed for buffering data between services in distributed systems. It supports both push and pull subscriptions, offering flexibility in how messages are delivered and processed. Push subscriptions enable real-time delivery to subscriber endpoints, which is ideal for immediate processing needs. Pull subscriptions allow subscribers to fetch messages at their own pace, suitable for batch processing or asynchronous workflows. Cloud Pub/Sub ensures reliable message delivery, scalability, and decoupling of components, making it a powerful tool for building resilient and scalable cloud architectures.

137. Answer: C

Explanation: Message queues help manage data flow between services, allowing for effective load balancing and handling service disruptions.

138. Answer: B

Explanation: Actionable alerts should convey clear and detailed information to DevOps engineers, enabling them to understand and promptly address issues. This includes providing context on the problem, its severity, relevant metrics, initial diagnostics, and actionable steps for resolution. By ensuring alerts are informative and actionable, teams can swiftly respond to incidents, minimize downtime, and maintain the reliability of systems and services.

139. Answer: C

Explanation: Cloud Dataflow is a fully managed service that implements the Apache Beam stream processing framework, suitable for stream and batch processing.

140. Answer: B

Explanation: When designing workflows, careful consideration of how data will flow between services is essential for achieving efficiency and reliability.

This includes defining clear data dependencies, understanding communication patterns, and choosing appropriate data transfer mechanisms. By ensuring streamlined data movement, workflows can operate smoothly, minimize bottlenecks, and maintain consistent performance across interconnected services.

141. Answer: C

Explanation: An instance template defines a machine type, boot disk image or container image, network settings, and other properties of a VM. It can be used to create single instances or manage groups of instances.

142. Answer: C

Explanation: Managed Instance Groups (MIGs) in Google Cloud Platform (GCP) indeed provide auto-healing capabilities by automatically restarting instances when the application does not respond as expected. This proactive feature helps maintain application availability and reliability by detecting issues such as instance failures or unresponsive applications and taking corrective action automatically. MIGs monitor the health of instances based on health checks defined by the user, ensuring that instances are continuously monitored and any issues are promptly addressed without manual intervention. This autohealing functionality is crucial for ensuring consistent performance and minimizing downtime in cloud environments.

143. Answer: C

Explanation: Compute Engine is suitable for running stateful applications like databases, providing customizable compute resources and persistent storage options.

144. Answer: C

Explanation: Canary updates indeed allow for running two versions of instance templates simultaneously to test a newer version before fully deploying it across the group. This deployment strategy involves directing a portion of incoming traffic or workload to instances using the new version while keeping the majority of traffic on instances using the current, stable version. This approach enables teams to validate changes, monitor performance, and ensure the new version operates correctly under real-world conditions before rolling it out completely. Canary updates are a common practice in software deployment to mitigate risks and ensure smooth transitions for updates or changes to production environments.

145. Answer: B

Explanation: App Engine Standard is a PaaS product that allows developers to run applications in a serverless environment, with restrictions on the programming languages used.

146. Answer: A

Explanation: The default instance class for applications running in App Engine Standard is F1, which has a 600 MHz CPU limit and 256 MB of memory.

147. Answer: B

Explanation: Compute Engine allows you to manage your disk encryption keys and provides options for highly secured environments.

148. Answer: B

Explanation: For high IOPS requirements, SSD persistent disks are recommended on Compute Engine instances due to their superior performance in read and write operations compared to standard persistent disks.

149. Answer: B

Explanation: App Engine Flexible supports running custom containers, providing a platform-as-a-service environment.

150. Answer: C

Explanation: Kubernetes Engine (GKE) leverages Compute Engine instance groups to deploy and manage Kubernetes clusters, providing robust container orchestration capabilities.

151. Answer: B

Explanation: Google Cloud Storage is designed for persisting unstructured data, such as data files, images, videos, and backup files. It treats these objects as atomic units without any presumed internal structure.

152. Answer: C

Explanation: It is recommended not to use personally identifying information in bucket names as it could be useful to an attacker. Other best practices include following DNS naming conventions, using GUIDs, and avoiding sequential names or timestamps.

153. Answer: B

Explanation: Multiregional storage mitigates the risk of a regional outage by storing replicas of objects in multiple regions, whereas Regional storage stores multiple copies of an object in multiple zones within a single region.

154. Answer: B

Explanation: In a rolling deployment, the new version of an application is gradually deployed to servers in small batches. This means that only a subset of the servers is updated at any given time while the others continue running the previous version. The process continues until all servers have been updated. This approach minimizes downtime and allows for easier rollback if issues are detected, as only a portion of the servers will be running the problematic code.

155. Answer: B

Explanation: Multiregional storage offers a 99.95% availability SLA, the highest among the storage classes for data stored in multiple regions. This high availability makes it ideal for storing frequently accessed data and ensuring data redundancy across geographically dispersed locations.

156. Answer: C

Explanation: Cloud Storage FUSE is an open-source adapter that allows users to mount Cloud Storage buckets as filesystems on Linux and MacOS platforms.

157. Answer: B

Explanation: Nearline storage is best suited for data that is accessed less than once in 30 days, providing a cost-effective solution for infrequently accessed data.

158. Answer: B

Explanation: Google Cloud Storage does not provide a native hierarchical directory structure. It treats objects as atomic units and uses a naming convention to simulate hierarchy.

159. Answer: B

Explanation: Google Cloud Storage is ideal for storing and sharing log files among multiple instances that do not need to be on persistent attached storage.

160. Answer: C

Explanation: Multiregional storage stores replicas of objects in multiple regions, which can improve access times and latency by distributing copies of objects to locations closer to the users.

161. Answer: B

Explanation: Google Cloud Filestore offers two tiers of service: Standard and Premium. These tiers differ in their performance characteristics, such as read/write throughput and IOPS.

162. Answer: B

Explanation: Cloud Filestore is commonly used for home directories, shared directories, web server content, and migrated applications that require a filesystem.

163. Answer: C

Explanation: The maximum read throughput for a 10+ TB Premium Cloud Filestore is 1.2 GB/s, as specified in its performance characteristics. This high throughput makes it suitable for applications requiring fast, large-scale data access and processing.

164. Answer: D

Explanation: The Cloud Filestore Editor role grants permissions to manage Cloud Filestore instances, including creating and deleting them. However, it does not provide full administrative permissions but allows for significant control over Cloud Filestore resources.

165. Answer: B

Explanation: Cloud Spanner supports horizontal scalability across regions and is designed for applications requiring strong consistency on a global scale. It provides a fully managed, scalable, and highly available database service with ACID transactions, making it ideal for mission-critical applications that need reliable and consistent data across multiple regions.

166. Answer: D

Explanation: Durability ensures that once a transaction is executed, the database state will permanently reflect the change, typically requiring the data to be written to persistent storage. This guarantees that committed transactions are not lost, even in the event of a system failure.

167. Answer: C

Explanation: Cloud SQL replicates data across multiple zones for high availability and manages failover to replicas.

168. Answer: C

Explanation: Cloud Spanner is used for applications requiring strong consistency on a global scale, such as financial trading systems, logistics applications, and global inventory tracking. Video streaming services are not typically a use case.

169. Answer: B

Explanation: Both the Standard and Premium tiers of Cloud Filestore have a typical availability of 99.9 percent.

170. Answer: C

Explanation: Cloud CDN (Content Delivery Network) is designed to improve the performance and availability of web applications and websites by caching static content at edge nodes located closer to users. This caching reduces latency because users can retrieve content from a nearby edge location rather than having to make requests all the way to the origin server.

171. Answer: C

Explanation: BigQuery is a managed data warehouse and analytics database solution in GCP designed to handle large volumes of data and perform complex aggregations. Cloud SQL and Cloud Spanner are relational databases, while Cloud Datastore is a NoSQL database.

172. Answer: B

Explanation: The 'bq head' command in BigQuery is used to list the first rows of a table, which helps users preview the structure and sample data of a table.

173. Answer: C

Explanation: The admin role in BigQuery grants permissions to perform all operations on BigQuery resources, providing complete control over the data and its management.

174. Answer: B

Explanation: BigQuery uses a columnar format to store values from a single column together, optimizing performance for analytics and business intelligence queries that often filter and group by specific columns.

175. Answer: B

Explanation: Cloud Bigtable is designed for storing and processing large-scale data, such as streaming IoT data, time series data, and other types of analytic operations.

176. Answer: C

Explanation: Cloud Datastore does not support joins, which are a common feature in relational databases. Instead, it uses a flexible document structure and supports a SQL-like query language called GQL.

177. Answer: B

Explanation: The --dry-run option in BigQuery provides an estimate of the number of bytes a query would return without actually executing the query, allowing users to gauge the potential cost and optimize their queries.

178. Answer: C

Explanation: Cloud Spanner is a relational database that supports horizontal scaling and is used when a single-server relational database is insufficient for transaction processing systems.

179. Answer: B

Explanation: BigQuery billing is based on the amount of data stored and the amount of data scanned when responding to queries, making it important to craft efficient queries to control costs.

180. Answer: A

Explanation: The 'mk' command in BigQuery is used to create new tables, views, and datasets, facilitating the organization and management of data within BigQuery projects.

181. Answer: B

Explanation: VPCs are used to organize Compute Engine instances, App Engine Flexible instances, and GKE clusters, and control network access to resources.

182. Answer: B

Explanation: While a VPC can span multiple regions, a VPC subnet is specific to a single region and provides private addresses to resources within that region.

183. Answer: C

Explanation: VPC network peering reduces the attack surface by making services in the VPC inaccessible from the public Internet.

184. Answer: B

Explanation: Shared VPC allows resources in different projects to communicate with each other while keeping the projects separate for organizational reasons.

185. Answer: C

Explanation: One of the implied firewall rules in Google Cloud allows all outgoing traffic from the VPC (Virtual Private Cloud). This rule ensures that any instance within the VPC can communicate with external resources without additional firewall configuration.

186. Answer: C

Explanation: VPC peering can connect VPCs between different organizations, whereas Shared VPC does not operate between organizations.

187. Answer: B

Explanation: The default network in a Google Cloud VPC includes four firewall rules: default-allow-internal (enabling internal communication between instances), default-allow-ssh (allowing SSH access on port 22), default-allow-RDP (allowing RDP access on port 3389), and default-allow-icmp (allowing ICMP traffic for diagnostics). These rules provide essential connectivity and management capabilities.

188. Answer: D

Explanation: To override the implied firewall rules in Google Cloud, you need to assign a priority value lower than 65535 to your custom firewall rules. Lower priority values take precedence, allowing you to define specific rules that can override the default behavior.

189. Answer: C

Explanation: Shared VPCs allow the separation of project and network management duties, offering more organizational flexibility.

190. Answer: B

Explanation: VPC network peering does not incur egress charges for traffic between peered networks within the same region, making it a cost-effective way to connect VPCs compared to using external IP addresses, which do incur egress charges.

191. Answer: C

Explanation: The default-allow-rdp firewall rule allows ingress connections on TCP port 3389 from any source to any instance in the network, enabling the use of Remote Desktop Protocol (RDP).

192. Answer: B

Explanation: All of the default firewall rules, including default-allow-ssh, default-allow-RDP, and default-allow-ICMP, have a priority of 65534, which is the second-lowest priority.

193. Answer: B

Explanation: The direction attribute in firewall rules specifies whether the traffic is ingress (inbound) or egress (outbound). This determines if the rule applies to incoming traffic to the network or outgoing traffic from the network.

194. Answer: A

Explanation: CIDR stands for Classless Inter-Domain Routing, a method used for allocating IP addresses and for efficient IP routing. It allows for a more flexible and efficient allocation of IP address space compared to the older class-based system.

195. Answer: C

Explanation: In a mirrored topology, the public cloud and private on-premise environments mirror each other, often for test or disaster recovery purposes.

196. Answer: B

Explanation: A hybrid-cloud environment is recommended for batch processing jobs that use custom legacy applications designed for mainframes, as these are best-run on-premises.

197. Answer: B

Explanation: In a gated egress topology, on-premises service APIs are made available to applications running in the cloud without exposing them to the public Internet.

198. Answer: C

Explanation: IPv4 addresses use four octets, formatted as four groups of numbers separated by periods, such as 192.168.20.10. Each octet can range from 0 to 255.

199. Answer: D

Explanation: A single network interconnect can become a single point of failure, which is a primary concern for reliability in a hybrid-cloud environment.

200. Answer: C

Explanation: In CIDR notation, the integer specifies the number of bits used to identify the subnet; the remaining bits are used to determine the host address.

201. Answer: A

Explanation: Cloud VPN is a GCP service that provides virtual private networks between GCP and on-premises networks using IPsec VPNs, supporting bandwidths up to 3 Gbps

202. Answer: B

Explanation: The primary advantage of using Cloud Interconnect over Cloud VPN is that Cloud Interconnect provides transmission of data over private connections, ensuring secure and reliable communication between your on-premises network and Google Cloud Platform. This contrasts with Cloud VPN, which relies on encrypted tunnels over the public internet.

203. Answer: C

Explanation: HTTP(S) Load Balancing is used for distributing HTTP and HTTPS traffic globally or across multiple regions. This helps ensure high availability, reliability, and optimal performance by directing traffic to the closest or most responsive backend services.

204. Answer: D

Explanation: TCP Proxy Load Balancing should be used for non-HTTPS and non-SSL traffic, providing a single IP address for all users globally.

205. Answer: C

Explanation: Cloud VPN uses the Internet Key Exchange (IKE) protocol to securely encrypt data at the origin gateway and decrypt it at the destination gateway. This ensures that data transmitted between networks over the public internet remains private and secure.

206. Answer: B

Explanation: Cloud VPN is less expensive and requires less management, making it suitable when low latency and high availability are not required.

207. Answer: B

Explanation: One of the disadvantages of using Cloud Interconnect is that it requires additional cost and complexity to manage compared to other networking options like Cloud VPN. This is due to the need for dedicated physical infrastructure and more involved configuration and operational overhead.

208. Answer: B

Explanation: The Internal TCP/UDP Load Balancer is indeed used to distribute workload across backend services that are running on Compute Engine instances with private IP addresses. It operates within a Virtual Private Cloud (VPC), providing internal load balancing for TCP and UDP traffic to ensure efficient and scalable communication between services within the same network. This load balancer helps optimize performance and reliability without exposing services to the public internet.

209. Answer: A

Explanation: SSL Proxy Load Balancer terminates SSL (Secure Sockets Layer) connections from clients and forwards unencrypted traffic to the backend instances. This offloading of SSL encryption and decryption tasks from backend instances helps in reducing the computational load on those instances, thereby improving their performance and scalability. This load balancer type is suitable for applications that handle HTTPS traffic and require SSL termination at the load balancer level before traffic is forwarded to backend instances.

210. Answer: B

Explanation: Cloud Interconnect allows for routing between networks by exchanging BGP (Border Gateway Protocol) routes. BGP is a standardized exterior gateway protocol that enables routers to exchange information and make decisions about the best paths for routing traffic between autonomous systems (ASes). Cloud Interconnect provides dedicated, low-latency connections between on-premises networks and Google Cloud Platform (GCP) networks, enabling private and secure data exchange. It supports both Layer 3 (IP) connectivity and Layer 2 (Ethernet) connectivity options, and it uses BGP to establish and maintain routing information across these connections. This makes it suitable for scenarios where low latency, high availability, and private connectivity are required between on-premises networks and GCP.

211. Answer: B

Explanation: The IAM service allows administrators to specify who gets to do what on which resources, controlling access to various GCP resources.

212. Answer: D

Explanation: A billing account is related to financial management and not an identity type. Google account, service account, and Cloud Identity domain are types of identities used to manage access in GCP.

213. Answer: A

Explanation: The Viewer role grants a user read-only permissions to a resource, enabling them to view but not modify the state of the resource. This role is useful for users who need to monitor or audit resources without making changes.

214. Answer: C

Explanation: In Google Cloud Platform (GCP) IAM, the naming convention for predefined roles follows the format `roles/service-name.role`. This structure helps identify roles by associating them with specific GCP services and their functionalities. It ensures clarity and organization in managing permissions across GCP environments.

215. Answer: C

Explanation: Custom roles allow users to create roles tailored to specific needs when predefined roles do not suffice.

216. Answer: B

Explanation: `compute.instances.get` is a permission related to Google Cloud's Compute Engine. It allows users to retrieve detailed information about virtual machine (VM) instances, including their configuration, status, and metadata. This permission is typically included in roles that provide read access to VM instances.

217. Answer: A

Explanation: Service accounts are used by applications running in Google Cloud Platform (GCP) to manage access controls and permissions, rather than using a person's account. These accounts allow applications and services to authenticate and interact with other GCP services securely, ensuring that permissions are appropriately managed and not tied to individual user accounts.

218. Answer: C

Explanation: The Owner role includes all the capabilities of the Editor role and additionally can manage roles and permissions for the resource. This means that an Owner can create, modify, and delete access controls, granting or revoking permissions as needed.

219. Answer: B

Explanation: Google Groups are collections of Google accounts and service accounts that can be used to grant permissions to multiple users simultaneously. This simplifies managing access controls by allowing permissions to be assigned to the group rather than individual accounts.

220. Answer: D

Explanation: The roles/bigquery.user role is suitable for a user who needs to query a database but does not perform administrative tasks.

221. Answer: B

Explanation: Explanation: The principle of least privilege ensures that a user is granted the minimum levels of access – or permissions – needed to perform their job functions, which is a security best practice.

222. Answer: B

Explanation: This role grants permissions related to managing and deploying Cloud Functions, including viewing and modifying the source code of Cloud Functions. It allows developers to work with the configuration, deployment, and monitoring aspects of Cloud Functions without requiring broader administrative access to IAM roles or policies, managing Cloud Storage buckets, or monitoring Cloud Audit Logs.

223. Answer: D

Explanation: If a developer should only be able to view the source code of Cloud Functions without the ability to change it, you should grant them the 'roles/cloudfunctions.viewer' role. This role specifically provides read-only access to Cloud Functions, allowing developers to inspect the configuration and source code but preventing them from making modifications.

224. Answer: C

Explanation: Policies in Google Cloud Identity and Access Management (IAM) are indeed specified using JSON format. These JSON policies define the permissions for users, groups, and service accounts, detailing which actions are allowed or denied on specific resources.

225. Answer: B

Explanation: The `setIamPolicy` function is used to set IAM policies on Google Cloud resources. This function allows you to define or update the access controls for a resource, specifying which users or service accounts have which permissions.

226. Answer: C

Explanation: Policies can be set anywhere in the resource hierarchy, including the organization, folder, project level, and individual resources.

227. Answer: C

Explanation: By granting roles to a group and then adding users to that group, you simplify management and ensure consistency in permissions. This approach streamlines the process of assigning and updating permissions, as changes to the group's roles automatically apply to all its members.

228. Answer: C

Explanation: Reviewing Cloud Audit Logs helps monitor changes to IAM policies. These logs provide detailed records of who made changes, what changes were made, and when they occurred, enhancing security and accountability in your Google Cloud environment.

229. Answer: B

Explanation: Google encrypts data at rest using Advanced Encryption Standard (AES) with 256-bit (AES256) and 128-bit (AES128) encryption standards. This ensures that data stored on Google's infrastructure is protected with strong encryption, maintaining data security and confidentiality.

230. Answer: B

Explanation: Envelope encryption involves encrypting data encryption keys (DEKs) with another key called the Key Encryption Key (KEK). This approach enhances security by separating the management of DEKs (used to encrypt data) from the encryption of those keys themselves. The KEK is typically stored securely and can be rotated more frequently than the DEKs, providing an additional layer of security for data encryption. This method ensures that even if DEKs are compromised, the data remains protected as long as the KEK remains secure.

231. Answer: C

Explanation: In Google Cloud Platform (GCP), new storage devices utilize AES256 encryption to encrypt blocks of data written to persistent storage. This encryption standard ensures that data stored on GCP's storage services is protected with strong encryption, enhancing data security and compliance with industry standards.

232. Answer: C

Explanation: The Google Front End (GFE) is a globally distributed proxy service provided by Google Cloud Platform. It acts as a front-end for HTTP and HTTPS traffic, terminating these protocols and then routing the traffic over Google's network to the backend servers running the application. This setup improves performance by leveraging Google's global infrastructure and enhances security through features like SSL termination and DDoS protection, making it ideal for scaling web applications globally.

233. Answer: C

Explanation: Within the Google Cloud infrastructure, Google uses Application Layer Transport Security (ALTS) for authentication and encryption at layer 7 of the OSI network model. ALTS ensures secure communication between services and applications within the Google network, protecting against unauthorized access and data interception. This approach helps maintain the confidentiality and integrity of data transmitted over Google's infrastructure.

234. Answer: B

Explanation: By default, DEKs are stored near the data chunks that they encrypt, and they are encrypted using Key Encryption Keys (KEKs) managed by a centralized key management service.

235. Answer: C

Explanation: Cloud KMS is a hosted key management service that allows customers to generate and store keys within GCP. It supports various cryptographic keys and provides functionality for key management.

236. Answer: C

Explanation: Customer-supplied keys offer the customer the greatest amount of control, as the keys are generated and stored on-premises and are used by GCP services to encrypt the customer's data.

237. Answer: B

Explanation: In Google Cloud Key Management Service (Cloud KMS), there is indeed a 24-hour delay before a KMS key is permanently destroyed. This delay is implemented to provide a safeguard in case the deletion is accidental or due to a malicious act. During this period, the key can be recovered or restored to prevent data loss. This feature helps ensure data security and integrity by allowing time for corrective actions before irreversible deletion occurs.

238. Answer: C

Explanation: The first phase of a penetration test is Reconnaissance, where testers gather information about the target system and the people who operate or have access to it.

239. Answer: C

Explanation: In the maintaining access phase, attackers will do things to hide their presence, such as manipulating logs or preventing attacking processes from appearing in a list of running

240. Answer: C

Explanation: Data in transit on the public Internet is encrypted by GCP to protect the confidentiality and integrity of the data if it is intercepted.

241. Answer: B

Explanation: While conducting a penetration test on the Google Cloud Platform (GCP), it's generally not required to notify Google beforehand. However, it's crucial to adhere strictly to GCP's terms of service and acceptable use policy. This ensures that the testing is conducted responsibly and within legal boundaries, avoiding any disruptions to Google's services or unintended consequences. Always review and comply with GCP's guidelines to maintain the security and reliability of both your infrastructure and Google's services.

242. Answer: C

Explanation: The Cloud Operations Logging Agent collects logs for widely used services, including Jenkins, MySQL, Redis, and more. It facilitates centralized logging and monitoring across various applications and infrastructure components, providing visibility into operational data and facilitating troubleshooting and analysis.

243. Answer: B

Explanation: Cloud Audit Logs is indeed a Google Cloud Platform (GCP) service that records administrative actions and data operations across various GCP services. It helps maintain a comprehensive audit trail by capturing events such as resource creation, modification, and deletion, as well as data access and configuration changes. This logging capability enhances security, compliance, and governance by providing visibility into activities that impact GCP resources and data.

244. Answer: C

Explanation: Logs are exported from Cloud Operations using methods like JSON files to Cloud Storage, logging tables to BigQuery datasets, and JSON messages to Cloud Pub/Sub.

245. Answer: C

Explanation: Least privilege is the cybersecurity principle of granting individuals or systems only the minimum permissions necessary to perform their required tasks or duties. This practice helps reduce the risk of unauthorized access, misuse, or accidental exposure of sensitive information or resources. By limiting permissions to what is essential for specific roles or functions, organizations can enhance security posture and mitigate potential security breaches or incidents.

246. Answer: C

Explanation: Separation of duties means limiting the responsibilities of a single individual, such as one person creating a bill and another paying it, to prevent fraud.

247. Answer: D

Explanation: The `roles/appengine.appAdmin` role grants permissions to read, write, and modify access to all application configurations and settings within Google App Engine. This role provides comprehensive administrative control over the configuration and settings of App Engine applications.

248. Answer: B

Explanation: Defense in depth is indeed the cybersecurity practice of employing multiple layers of security controls to protect resources and data. By implementing a diverse range of security measures across networks, systems, applications, and data, organizations can create overlapping layers of defense. This approach ensures that if one security control is breached or fails, other layers remain intact to mitigate the impact and prevent further unauthorized access or damage. Defense in depth is essential for enhancing overall cybersecurity resilience and reducing the likelihood of successful cyberattacks.

249. Answer: B

Explanation: To meet regulations that require longer retention periods, audit logs should be exported from Cloud Audit Logs to Cloud Storage or BigQuery.

250. Answer: B

Explanation: The primitive roles, such as roles/viewer, roles/editor, and roles/owner, are not suitable for implementing the principle of least privilege because they grant broad permissions.

251. Answer: B

Explanation: Phishing schemes often involve tricking users into providing their login credentials, which attackers can then use to bypass authentication systems.

252. Answer: C

Explanation: By setting firewall rules to only allow traffic from trusted IP addresses, the attacker would be unable to access the resource from untrusted IPs.

253. Answer: C

Explanation: The Heartbleed vulnerability was found in OpenSSL, allowing attackers to read memory from servers or clients using the compromised version.

254. Answer: B

Explanation: These regulations aim to protect individuals' privacy and ensure the security of business information within the realm of information technology. They often include guidelines and requirements for data protection, secure handling of personal information, and measures to safeguard sensitive business data from unauthorized access or breaches. Examples of such regulations may include GDPR (General Data Protection Regulation) in Europe or CCPA (California Consumer Privacy Act) in the United States, among others, which impose legal obligations on organizations to uphold privacy and security standards in handling data.

255. Answer: C

Explanation: While Google is responsible for protecting the physical infrastructure and lower levels of the GCP platform, customers are responsible for application-level security.

256. Answer: C

Explanation: The HIPAA Privacy Rule grants patients the right to review information in their records and request information.

257. Answer: B

Explanation: The HIPAA Security Rule requires organizations to ensure the confidentiality, integrity, and availability of healthcare information and to protect against expected threats and unauthorized disclosures.

258. Answer: C

Explanation: The HITECH Act, enacted in 2009, includes rules governing the transmission of health information and extends HIPAA (Health Insurance Portability and Accountability Act) regulations to business associates. This legislation aims to strengthen the privacy and security of health information by imposing stricter requirements and penalties for violations. It mandates that organizations handling health data, including healthcare providers and their business associates, comply with enhanced standards for electronic health records (EHR) and safeguard patient information against unauthorized access and breaches.

259. Answer: D

Explanation: The General Data Protection Regulation (GDPR) applies to individuals living in the European Union and aims to protect their data.

260. Answer: B

Explanation: The HIPAA Security Rule requires organizations to have comprehensive security measures, including management practices, access control, incident response, and contingency planning.

261. Answer: D

Explanation: All of the listed services (Compute Engine, App Engine, Kubernetes Engine) are covered under Google's Business Associate Agreement (BAA. for HIPAA) compliance.

262. Answer: B

Explanation: Under GDPR (General Data Protection Regulation), the controller is responsible for obtaining and managing the consent of individuals whose data is collected. This includes ensuring that consent is freely given, specific, informed, and unambiguous. Controllers must also provide individuals with clear information about how their data will be used, processed, and protected. Additionally, they are responsible for enabling individuals to withdraw consent at any time if they choose to do so. These responsibilities are part of GDPR's framework for ensuring the privacy rights of individuals and promoting transparent and lawful data processing practices.

263. Answer: A

Explanation: Data processors must notify the controller in the event of a data breach under GDPR. The controller is then responsible for notifying the supervising authority and the individuals affected.

264. Answer: B

Explanation: SOX, or the Sarbanes-Oxley Act of 2002, is indeed designed to protect the public from fraudulent accounting practices in publicly traded companies. It was enacted in response to corporate accounting scandals, such as Enron and WorldCom, to improve transparency, accountability, and governance within these companies. SOX imposes stringent requirements on financial reporting and internal controls, aiming to restore investor confidence and prevent future financial misconduct. It mandates measures such as CEO and CFO certification of financial statements, independent audits, and stricter penalties for fraudulent activities to enhance corporate accountability and protect stakeholders' interests.

265. Answer: D

Explanation: COPPA primarily emphasizes obtaining verifiable parental consent before collecting personal information from children under the age of 13 on websites and online services. While the law promotes securing children's data, it does not explicitly mandate encryption of all collected data as a requirement.

266. Answer: C

Explanation: Incident management is indeed a core component of ITIL (Information Technology Infrastructure Library) service management practices rather than general management practices. It focuses on promptly resolving disruptions or incidents in IT services to minimize the impact on business operations and ensure service continuity. Incident management within ITIL involves processes for logging, categorizing, prioritizing, and resolving incidents efficiently, often employing predefined procedures and escalation paths to restore services swiftly. This structured approach helps organizations maintain high levels of service availability and customer satisfaction by effectively managing and mitigating the impact of IT incidents.

267. Answer: B

Explanation: SOX requires companies to enforce access controls to protect the integrity of financial data, ensuring it remains accurate and secure from unauthorized access or tampering. These controls are critical for maintaining transparency and reliability in financial reporting practices.

268. Answer: C

Explanation: COPPA (Children's Online Privacy Protection Act) primarily focuses on safeguarding the online privacy of children under the age of 13. It imposes requirements on websites and online services that collect personal information from children, aiming to ensure parental consent, limit data collection, and maintain the security and confidentiality of children's information online.

269. Answer: B

Explanation: Organizations adopt ITIL (Information Technology Infrastructure Library) to establish consistent and repeatable best practices that encompass both business and technical domains. This framework helps improve service delivery, efficiency, and alignment with business goals by providing structured guidelines for managing IT services. By implementing ITIL practices, organizations can enhance operational effectiveness, mitigate risks, and achieve greater overall IT service management maturity.

270. Answer: D

Explanation: Financial management practices are indeed not specifically listed as a practice area under ITIL (Information Technology Infrastructure Library). ITIL primarily focuses on service management practices related to delivering and managing IT services effectively. However, financial management for IT services is often addressed within broader ITIL practices, such as service strategy and service design, where considerations like budgeting, cost management, and financial planning for IT services are integrated into overall service management frameworks.

271. Answer: C

Explanation: In short, Cloud Operations Monitoring (Google Cloud's Operations suite) is used to collect and monitor metrics and telemetry data from Google Cloud services and applications. It helps track the health, performance, and availability of infrastructure and applications hosted on Google Cloud Platform.

272. Answer: D

Explanation: Cloud Operations consists of Monitoring, Logging, and Alerting services. Deployment is not a component of Cloud Operations.

273. Answer: B

Explanation: A time series is a set of metrics recorded at specific intervals with associated time stamps, showing how a particular metric changes over time.

274. Answer: C

Explanation: A dropping cache hit ratio indicates that the memory size is insufficient, causing more data to be read from persistent storage, which increases latency.

275. Answer: B

Explanation: The goal of alerting is to notify responsible parties when specific conditions are met, indicating an incident or issue that needs human intervention.

276. Answer: C

Explanation: To minimize false alerts, it is important to experiment and find the optimal threshold that balances between catching real issues and avoiding unnecessary notifications.

277. Answer: C

Explanation: Metrics are measurements that provide insights into various properties of infrastructure and applications, such as CPU utilization or network traffic.

278. Answer: B

Explanation: Dashboards provide visual displays of time series data, which can help in diagnosing problems and identifying correlated failures within the system.

279. Answer: B

Explanation: Conditions in alerting policies are rules that determine when a resource is considered unhealthy and an alert should be triggered.

280. Answer: C

Explanation: Cloud Operations Monitoring helps maintain cost-efficient services by providing detailed insights into application and infrastructure performance, allowing for optimization and resource management.

281. Answer: A

Explanation: "Alert fatigue" occurs when engineers are overwhelmed by a high volume of unnecessary or low-priority alerts, leading to a desensitization towards alerts. This can result in critical alerts being ignored or missed because they are buried among numerous less important notifications. This phenomenon reduces the effectiveness of the alerting system and can lead to significant issues being overlooked.

282. Answer: C

Explanation: Reliability in Compute Engine can be significantly improved by automatically responding to changes in workload or other conditions. This can be achieved through features like auto-scaling and managed instance groups, which automatically adjust the number of VM instances based on current demand. This ensures that applications can handle varying loads efficiently and maintain high availability.

283. Answer: B

Explanation: One significant advantage of using managed services like BigQuery over running a relational database in Compute Engine is that it eliminates the need to monitor and manage servers. Managed services handle infrastructure management, scaling, and maintenance, allowing you to focus on data analysis and application development without worrying about underlying server operations. While cost, performance, and engineering resources can also be factors, the primary benefit here is the reduced operational overhead from not having to monitor and manage the servers directly.

284. Answer: B

Explanation: A key feature of Cloud Operations Logging is its ability to store logs from virtually any application or resource, not just those within the Google Cloud Platform (GCP). This flexibility allows organizations to centralize their logging infrastructure and analyze logs from various environments, including on-premises systems, other cloud platforms, and third-party applications.

285. Answer: C

Explanation: By default, Cloud Operations Logging retains log messages for 30 days. This retention period allows users to review and analyze recent log data while managing storage costs and performance. For longer retention, logs can be exported to services like Cloud Storage or BigQuery.

286. Answer: B

Explanation: To keep logs for longer than the default retention period in Cloud Operations Logging, you can export them to Cloud Storage or BigQuery. This allows for extended retention, further analysis, and compliance with data retention policies.

287. Answer: D

Explanation: Cloud Operations Logging offers text searching, structured SQL-based analysis via BigQuery, and integration with Cloud Operations Alerting for efficient log management and monitoring within the Google Cloud Platform. However, it does not provide automatic bug-fixing capabilities.

288. Answer: B

Explanation: Events that might trigger log messages include critical incidents like database connection errors, which are crucial for system monitoring and troubleshooting. These logs help maintain system reliability by recording significant events and issues that impact application functionality and performance.

289. Answer: A

Explanation: Cloud Operations provides monitoring, alerting, and log management tools. Monitoring tracks performance metrics, alerting notifications based on thresholds, and log management centralizes log data for analysis, ensuring efficient service management in the Google Cloud Platform.

290. Answer: B

Explanation: Streaming logs to Cloud Pub/Sub enables near real-time operations because Cloud Pub/Sub is a fully managed, real-time messaging service that allows for the asynchronous, reliable delivery of messages between applications. By streaming logs to Cloud Pub/Sub, organizations can process and analyze log data in real-time or near real-time, enabling rapid detection and response to operational events and issues. This approach facilitates timely monitoring, troubleshooting, and decision-making based on current system and application performance data.

291. Answer: C

Explanation: Release management helps in deploying code frequently and with small changes, allowing developers to get fixes out faster and reducing the risk of introducing new bugs.

292. Answer: B

Explanation: Continuous Deployment (CD) is a software engineering approach where code changes are automatically tested and deployed to production environments frequently, typically several times a day or more. This practice ensures that any code change that passes automated tests is immediately deployed to production, minimizing the time between writing new code and making that code available to users. It aims to achieve rapid, reliable, and frequent delivery of updates to applications.

293. Answer: C

Explanation: Continuous deployment favors the rapid release of code, which can increase the risk of bugs if not thoroughly tested automatically.

294. Answer: C

Explanation: Teams that need to ensure a low risk of bugs or are not proficient at writing automated tests may opt for continuous delivery, which includes human review before deployment.

295. Answer: D

Explanation: Unit tests are designed to find bugs within the smallest units of code, such as functions or API endpoints.

296. Answer: C

Explanation: Acceptance tests are designed to assure business owners that the code meets the business requirements of the system.

297. Answer: B

Explanation: Integration tests check combinations of units to ensure they function well together, catching bugs that unit tests might miss.

298. Answer: D

Explanation: Load testing creates workloads for the system to understand its performance under particular conditions, such as heavy load.

299. Answer: B

Explanation: Continuous deployment involves writing comprehensive tests to automatically detect bugs early, as there is no human review before code release.

300. Answer: B

Explanation: Release management tools capture standardized release procedures and best practices over time, which helps in improving overall reliability.

301. Answer: C

Explanation: System tests include all integrated components and test whether an entire system functions as expected. They start with simple "sanity checks" and proceed to performance and regression tests.

302. Answer: C

Explanation: Sanity checks determine whether all of the components function under the simplest conditions before additional load is introduced.

303. Answer: D

Explanation: Regression tests are designed to ensure that bugs that have been corrected in the past are not reintroduced to the system at a later time.

304. Answer: B

Explanation: Reliability stress tests place increasing loads on a system until it breaks to understand failures and their cascading effects.

305. Answer: B

Explanation: Chaos engineering, exemplified by tools like Netflix's Simian Army, introduces failures randomly into functioning systems to study the impact and improve system resilience.

306. Answer: B

Explanation: Incidents are events that have a significant adverse impact on a service's ability to function and affect multiple internal teams or external customers.

307. Answer: B

Explanation: The incident commander is responsible for coordinating the response to an incident, ensuring effective communication and decision-making.

308. Answer: B

Explanation: The main focus of incident management is to correct problems and restore services to customers or other system users as soon as possible.

309. Answer: B

Explanation: Post-mortem analysis aims to identify the causes of an incident, understand why it happened, and determine measures to prevent it from happening again.

310. **Answer: B**

Explanation: It's important that post-mortem analyses do not assign blame primarily to foster a culture of trust and honesty within teams. Blameless analyses encourage open communication, systemic issue identification, and effective solutions for preventing future incidents.

311. **Answer: B**

Explanation: The Analysis phase focuses on understanding the problem, evaluating options for solving it, and assessing the cost-benefit of various options.

312. **Answer: D**

Explanation: Buying COTS software does not allow full control over architecture and systems design choices; this is an advantage of building from scratch.

313. **Answer: B**

Explanation: High-level design involves identifying the major subcomponents of a system and defining their interfaces. This phase focuses on the overall structure and interactions between the system's key components, setting the stage for detailed design and implementation. It provides a blueprint for how the system's parts will work together to meet the specified requirements.

314. Answer: C

Explanation: RESTful interfaces are commonly used with microservices to enable communication between components.

315. Answer: B

Explanation: The Design phase involves high-level and detailed design to map out how the software will be structured and how key functions will be implemented.

316. Answer: B

Explanation: Evaluating whether to buy or build a solution is indeed a critical consideration during the Analysis phase. This evaluation involves assessing the project's requirements, budget, timeline, and available resources to determine if it's more feasible and cost-effective to purchase an existing solution or develop a custom one in-house. The decision impacts the project's overall strategy, including future maintenance, scalability, and integration with other systems.

317. Answer: B

Explanation: Cost-benefit analysis helps in comparing the relative value of different project options, including financial and opportunity costs.

318. Answer: B

Explanation: Detailed design focuses on decomposing components into modules and defining the specific details of data structures, algorithms, security controls, and user interfaces. This phase involves creating comprehensive specifications for each module, ensuring that all parts of the system are designed to work together seamlessly and meet the requirements outlined in the high-level design. It provides a clear roadmap for developers to implement the system accurately and efficiently.

319. Answer: B

Explanation: High licensing costs and the inability to customize the software are indeed potential disadvantages of buying software. Purchased software often comes with significant licensing fees, which can be expensive, especially for large organizations. Additionally, off-the-shelf software may not meet all specific business requirements. It may lack the flexibility for customization, limiting its ability to adapt to unique workflows or integrate with other systems seamlessly.

320. Answer: B

Explanation: Modifying an existing application often allows leveraging of existing code, infrastructure, and knowledge, which can significantly reduce development time and effort compared to starting from scratch. This approach can expedite deployment and time-to-market for solutions or improvements.

321. Answer: B

Explanation: CI/CD allows new features to be rolled out quickly for use by customers, making it a practical option for modern software deployment.

322. Answer: B

Explanation: Operations documentation includes instructions used by system administrators and DevOps engineers to deploy and maintain system operations.

323. Answer: A

Explanation: Unit testing and integration testing are commonly performed during the development phase to ensure that individual components and their interactions work correctly.

324. Answer: C

Explanation: Version control systems, such as GitHub and Cloud Source Repositories, are used to support collaboration among developers.

325. Answer: C

Explanation: Monitoring collects data on application and infrastructure performance, providing developers visibility into how their applications are functioning.

326. Answer: C

Explanation: In agile development environments, user documentation should be updated frequently to keep pace with the rapid changes in system features.

327. Answer: C

Explanation: A runbook includes instructions on how to set up and run a service or application and may contain troubleshooting advice as well.

328. Answer: C

Explanation: Safety-critical systems may require rigorous validation procedures that include human review, making CI/CD inappropriate sometimes.

329. Answer: B

Explanation: Feature flags are used to selectively release new capabilities to customers, allowing for controlled rollouts of new features.

330. Answer: C

Explanation: Architects have substantial roles in the early phases of the SDLC, including setting standards for tools like version-controlled systems and CI/CD platforms.

331. Answer: B

Explanation: Chaos engineering is the practice of introducing failures into a system to better understand the consequences of those failures and identify unanticipated failure modes.

332. Answer: C

Explanation: Netflix's Simian Army is a collection of chaos engineering tools that introduce failures at various levels of infrastructure, from instances to availability zones.

333. Answer: C

Explanation: The first thing to do in a major incident is to restore service, which may involve several people with different responsibilities, such as software developers, network engineers, and database administrators.

VERSAtile Reads

334. Answer: B

Explanation: The goal of the review is to understand what happened, why it happened, and how it could be prevented in the future. It is not about assigning blame.

335. Answer: B

Explanation: A major incident occurs when a large portion of users are adversely affected by a disruption in service, or there is a loss of data.

336. Answer: C

Explanation: One key element of post-mortem culture is to learn as much as possible from failures, whether they are minor or major incidents.

337. Answer: C

Explanation: An incident post-mortem is a review of the causes of an incident, an assessment of the effectiveness of responses to the incident, and discussions of lessons learned.

338. Answer: C

Explanation: One remediation could be to develop a static code analysis script that checks that parameter names are all in a list of valid parameter names.

339. Answer: B

Explanation: Project post-mortems are reviews of a project that help improve team practices and identify issues that might have slowed down work or caused problems for team members.

340. Answer: C

Explanation: A blameless culture means engineers should feel free to disclose mistakes without fear of retribution, understanding that complex systems fail even when everyone does their best.

341. Answer: B

Explanation: ITIL stands for Information Technology Infrastructure Library, which is a set of service management practices used to plan and execute IT operations.

342. Answer: C

Explanation: The four dimensions of the ITIL model are Organizations and people, Information and technology products, Partners and suppliers, and Value streams and processes.

343. Answer: A

Explanation: General management practices in ITIL include strategy management, portfolio management, and architecture management. These practices help organizations align IT services with business goals, manage the IT service portfolio effectively, and ensure that IT architecture supports the overall business strategy.

344. Answer: B

Explanation: Business continuity planning aims to keep the business operating during large-scale disruptions such as natural disasters.

345. Answer: C

Explanation: A disaster plan includes strategies for responding to a disaster, such as establishing operations, prioritizing services, and dealing with suppliers and insurance carriers.

346. Answer: B

Explanation: A business impact analysis (BIA) typically includes assessing the possible outcomes of different disaster scenarios and estimating the costs associated with various response strategies. The purpose of a BIA is to identify and prioritize critical business functions and processes, understand their dependencies on IT systems and infrastructure, and quantify the potential financial and operational impacts of disruptions. By conducting a BIA, organizations can develop effective disaster recovery and continuity plans to mitigate risks and ensure business resilience.

347. Answer: B

Explanation: The recovery plan outlines the specific steps and procedures required to restore services to normal operations after a disruption. This plan includes details on how to recover IT systems, applications, and infrastructure, as well as the sequence of actions to be taken. It also defines recovery time objectives (RTOs), which specify the maximum acceptable downtime for each system or service before its restoration is considered complete. The recovery plan ensures that organizations can respond promptly and effectively to incidents, minimizing the impact on business operations and maintaining service availability.

348. Answer: B

Explanation: Disaster recovery focuses specifically on IT operations and includes planning for deploying services in environments other than the usual production environment.

349. Answer: C

Explanation: DR (Disaster Recovery) plans should include provisions to ensure that access controls in the DR environment are consistent with those in the normal production environment. This consistency is crucial for maintaining security and compliance standards during a disaster or disruption. By aligning access controls, organizations can prevent unauthorized access to sensitive data and resources, uphold regulatory requirements, and ensure the continuity of secure operations across both environments. This helps mitigate risks associated with potential security breaches or data breaches during recovery efforts.

350. Answer: B

Explanation: Testing DR plans is crucial to verify that they are effective and can be executed as planned during an actual disaster situation.

351. Answer: B

Explanation: The first stage of stakeholder management is identifying stakeholders. This involves recognizing all individuals or groups who have a stake in the project.

352. Answer: B

Explanation: An information security engineer has significant influence over the release of code if it contains security vulnerabilities, as ensuring security compliance is part of their role.

353. Answer: C

Explanation: Interest refers to what a stakeholder wants from the project, while influence refers to their power to affect the project's outcomes.

354. Answer: D

Explanation: The forms of stakeholder interests mentioned are financial, organizational, and personnel. Geographical interests are not listed as a form of stakeholder interest in the provided context.

355. Answer: C

Explanation: A senior vice president responsible for a portfolio has both interests and significant influence over all projects and programs within that portfolio.

356. Answer: A

Explanation: Functional interests are related to the specific functions or features that stakeholders want in the project, such as API functions desired by a team of engineers.

357. Answer: B

Explanation: Determining roles and scope of interests involves collaborating with program and project managers to identify all stakeholders and understand their interests.

358. Answer: C

Explanation: A project is a focused initiative with a specific goal, budget, and schedule. It is managed within defined constraints to achieve its objectives efficiently.

359. Answer: C

Explanation: A communication plan is crucial for maintaining effective communication with stakeholders and influencing them as needed throughout the project.

360. Answer: B

Explanation: A compliance officer's scope of interest is focused on ensuring that the project complies with regulatory requirements, particularly around privacy and security.

361. Answer: B

Explanation: The communication plan can include various methods, such as publishing updates to a project site or holding regular status update meetings to keep stakeholders informed.

362. Answer: C

Explanation: Architects need to influence stakeholders to advocate for key technical decisions and demonstrate that proposed approaches are the best options for the project.

363. Answer: B

Explanation: Successful digital transformation efforts often include knowledgeable leaders, the ability to build workforce capabilities, enabling new ways of working, and good communications.

364. Answer: C

Explanation: The Plan-Do-Study-Act methodology developed by Walter Shewhart and popularized by W. Edwards Deming is discussed as a method for managing change.

365. Answer: C

Explanation: In the 'Plan' stage, the change experiment is developed, predictions are made, and various possible results are outlined.

366. Answer: C

Explanation: Technology-driven changes, such as the advent of autonomous vehicles, require enterprises to adapt to new technologies and skills.

367. Answer: C

Explanation: Enabling new ways of working is a common trait in successful digital transformation efforts, along with knowledgeable leadership and good communication.

368. Answer: B

Explanation: During the 'Study' stage, results are compared to the predictions, and other learning opportunities are identified.

369. Answer: C

Explanation: Externally motivated changes for individuals include changes such as a company reorganizing, a colleague leaving a team, or collaborators being moved to a new office.

370. Answer: C

Explanation: The purpose of a whitepaper posted by an architect is to make business owners aware of key technical decisions while demonstrating to engineers that the proposed approach is the best option for the project.

371. Answer: B

Explanation: Architects typically do not provide direct customer support for service issues; customer support teams more commonly handle this. Their responsibilities include defining skills, identifying gaps, and mentoring.

372. Answer: C

Explanation: The main objective of customer success management is to advance the business goals by ensuring customers gain value from the products and services offered.

373. Answer: B

Explanation: Customer acquisition is the practice of engaging new customers, which starts with identifying potential customers.

374. Answer: B

Explanation: Architects are not typically involved in customer acquisition, which is more related to marketing and sales efforts.

375. Answer: C

Explanation: Resource planning is the first step in cost management, where projects and programs requiring funding are identified and prioritized.

376. Answer: B

Explanation: The main types of costs in cost estimating include human resources, infrastructure, operational, and capital costs.

377. Answer: C

Explanation: Cost budgeting is the stage where decisions are made about how to allocate funds to maximize overall benefits to the organization.

378. Answer: C

Explanation: Professional services involve consulting services where customers may need help integrating new software or services with their existing systems.

379. Answer: B

Explanation: Resource planning involves identifying, prioritizing, and allocating resources across projects to ensure efficient utilization and achievement of organizational goals.

380. Answer: B

Explanation: Cost control is part of cost management, not customer success management. The four stages of customer success management are customer acquisition, marketing and sales, professional services, and training and support.

381. Answer: A

Explanation: HTTP status code 200 indicates a successful response from a server to a client's request. It signifies that the request has been successfully processed, and the server is returning the requested resource or action to the client. This status code is commonly used in various web-based APIs and services to indicate that the operation was completed successfully without any errors.

382. Answer: C

Explanation: HTTP status code 400 indicates a "Bad Request," which occurs when the server cannot process the request due to a client error. This can happen if the request contains invalid arguments, malformed syntax, or incorrect parameters. Essentially, it means the server received the request but found it to be invalid or incomprehensible, preventing it from being fulfilled.

383. Answer: B

Explanation: API keys are strings of alphanumeric characters that uniquely identify a user to a service and perform basic authentication.

384. Answer: B

Explanation: The payload of a JWT (JSON Web Token) contains a set of claims. These claims provide information about the token, such as the issuer (iss), the subject (sub), and various other pieces of data. Claims can be registered, public, or private, and they help to convey the necessary information about the token's authentication context and intended use.

385. Answer: B

Explanation: Rate limiting sets a maximum rate of API calls to control resource usage, such as limiting a user to 100 API calls a minute.

386. Answer: C

Explanation: HTTPS provides encryption to protect data in transit between a client and an API endpoint. By using HTTPS, the data exchanged is encrypted using Transport Layer Security (TLS), which ensures that the information is secure and cannot be easily intercepted or tampered with by unauthorized parties. This encryption is critical for maintaining the confidentiality and integrity of the data during transmission.

387. Answer: C

Explanation: Data-driven testing uses structured data sets with defined input values and expected output values to drive tests.

388. Answer: C

Explanation: The signature in a JWT (JSON Web Token) is the output of a cryptographic signature algorithm. This signature is generated using the encoded header, encoded payload, and a secret key (or a private key in the case of asymmetric algorithms). The purpose of the signature is to ensure the integrity and authenticity of the token, allowing the recipient to verify that the token has not been altered and that a trusted source issued it.

389. Answer: C

Explanation: Predefined roles in IAM are designed to accommodate common requirements for different types of users of services.

390. Answer: B

Explanation: HTTP status code 404 indicates that the requested resource was not found on the server. This status code is returned when the server cannot find the requested resource, either because it does not exist or it has been moved or deleted without providing a forwarding address. It signifies that the client was able to communicate with the server, but the server could not locate the specified resource.

391. Answer: B

Explanation: The assessment phase involves taking an inventory of applications and infrastructure, documenting considerations for moving each application to the cloud, and identifying each application's dependencies on other applications and data.

392. Answer: C

Explanation: The pilot phase involves migrating one or two applications to learn about the cloud, develop experience in running applications in the cloud, and understand the effort required for setup.

393. Answer: B

Explanation: For applications that require high availability, it is crucial to consider the recovery time objectives and locations of failover databases as part of the migration plan.

394. Answer C

Explanation: After the data has been migrated, the application migration phase involves moving applications to the cloud, either using a lift-and-shift model or transitioning to containers.

395. Answer: C

Explanation: The optimization phase focuses on improving the cloud implementation, which includes adding monitoring and logging tools like Cloud Operations to enhance application performance and reliability.

396. Answer: D

Explanation: Applications that are scheduled to be removed from service soon, such as a legacy application on a mainframe, are not good candidates for cloud migration.

397. Answer: C

Explanation: During the data migration phase, if data is being updated, you will need to develop a way to synchronize the on-premises data with the cloud data after the bulk of data has been migrated.

398. Answer: C

Explanation: During the optimization phase, third-party ETL tools can be replaced by GCP services such as Cloud Dataflow to streamline data processing and management.

399. Answer: B

Explanation: Documenting the production level and SLAs of an application helps in understanding its criticality, compliance needs, and the risk involved in migrating it to the cloud.

400. Answer: C

Explanation: Applications that must be available 24/7 and risk significant adverse impacts on the business if disrupted are categorized as Tier 1, indicating their high criticality in the migration planning process.

401. Answer: B

Explanation: It's important to verify if an on-premises license can be moved to the cloud or converted to a cloud license due to potential restrictions that limit its use to on-premises infrastructures.

402. Answer: C

Explanation: When migrating an on-premises application with a single site license to run in multiple regions in the cloud, it's crucial to consider whether the existing single site license permits such multi-region deployment. Software licenses often specify limitations on the geographic scope of use, such as single-site or single-region licenses. Deploying the application across multiple regions without the appropriate license could violate licensing terms and potentially lead to legal issues. Therefore, ensuring that the license is suitable for multi-region use is essential to avoid compliance risks and legal liabilities.

403. Answer: D

Explanation: The components of VPCs include networks, subnets, IP addresses, routes, and VPNs. Firewalls are part of network access controls, not VPC components.

404. Answer: B

Explanation: Cloud Load Balancing can distribute traffic and workloads globally using a single anycast IP address. This capability allows it to efficiently route client requests to the nearest or most optimal backend, enhancing performance, reducing latency, and improving reliability by balancing the load across multiple regions and resources.

405. Answer: C

Explanation: VPNs are provided by the Cloud VPN service that links your Google Cloud VPC to an on-premises network.

406. Answer: D

Explanation: The Network Admin role in Google Cloud provides full permissions to manage network resources. This role allows the user to create, modify, and delete network-related resources such as virtual private clouds (VPCs), subnets, firewalls, routes, and VPNs, ensuring comprehensive control over the network infrastructure.

407. Answer: B

Explanation: Network load balancing occurs at Layer 4 of the OSI model and is useful for dealing with spikes in TCP and IP traffic. It distributes traffic based on information in the transport layer, such as TCP/UDP ports and IP addresses, ensuring efficient handling of large volumes of traffic and improving the performance and reliability of applications.

408. Answer: C

Explanation: Static IP addresses are used when you need a consistent long-term IP address, such as for a public website or API endpoint.

409. Answer: C

Explanation: CDN Interconnect provides direct access to Google's edge network. It allows content delivery network (CDN) providers to connect directly with Google's infrastructure, resulting in lower latency, improved performance, and reduced egress costs for content delivered to users.

410. Answer: B

Explanation: Custom routes can be created if you need to implement many-to-one NAT or transparent proxies within a VPC.

411. Answer: B

Explanation: Ward Cunningham coined the term "Technical Debt" to describe the process of making reasonable choices to meet an objective, such as releasing code by a particular date. This concept highlights the trade-offs between short-term gains and long-term code quality and maintainability.

412. Answer: B

Explanation: Overstaffing a project is not listed as a reason for incurring technical debt. The reasons include insufficient understanding of requirements, the need to deliver on time or within budget, poor collaboration, lack of coding standards, and insufficient testing.

413. Answer: C

Explanation: Ideally, technical debt is paid down by refactoring code and implementing a better solution. Refactoring involves restructuring existing code to improve its readability, maintainability, and efficiency without changing its external behavior. By addressing technical debt through refactoring and implementing better solutions, teams can reduce complexity, enhance code quality, and mitigate risks associated with maintaining legacy or hastily developed codebases. This approach supports long-term sustainability and agility in software development projects.

414. Answer: B

Explanation: Architectural design debt is incurred when an architecture design choice is made for expedience but will require rework later.

415. Answer: D

Explanation: Environment debt occurs when expedient choices are made around tooling, such as manual builds and tests, instead of setting up a CI/CD platform.

416. Answer: B

Explanation: One of the first things to do in the next phase is to revise the code to improve error handling and perform thorough code reviews.

417. Answer: C

Explanation: In a REST API, the Create method typically uses HTTP POST to create an object or resource on the server. When a client sends a POST request to a specific endpoint (e.g., `/API/resource`), it includes the data for the new object in the request body. The server processes this request, creates the object based on the provided data, assigns it a unique identifier, and returns a response indicating the success or failure of the operation, along with any relevant metadata about the newly created resource.

418. Answer: B

Explanation: Simple resources in the context of RESTful APIs typically consist of a single entity or object. These resources represent a discrete unit of data or information that can be accessed, manipulated, and represented through API endpoints. Simple resources are straightforward in structure and often correspond directly to a single database record or a logical unit of information within an application. They are fundamental building blocks for designing RESTful APIs that expose specific functionalities and data to client applications.

419. Answer: D

Explanation: In a RESTful API, the Delete operation uses the HTTP DELETE method to remove or delete a resource identified by a specific URI (Uniform Resource Identifier). When a client sends a DELETE request to the server for a particular resource (e.g., `/API/resource/123`), the server processes this request to delete the resource associated with the identifier `123`. After successful deletion, the server typically responds with a status code indicating the success of the operation (e.g., HTTP status code 204 No Content) or with a relevant message confirming the deletion.

420. Answer: C

Explanation: Not paying down technical debt can lead to issues in production that negatively affect users, such as less reliable applications and missed bugs.

421. Answer: A

Explanation: A test is defined as a sequence of steps to execute, such as the steps to enter a new customer into a database.

422. Answer: B

Explanation: Data for each test is stored in another document or data source, such as a spreadsheet, which contains example names, addresses, phone numbers, and email addresses.

423. Answer: B

Explanation: In model-based testing, a simulation program is used to generate test data, often built in parallel with the system under test.

424. Answer: B

Explanation: Test-driven development (TDD) incorporates testing into the development process by mapping requirements to specific, narrowly scoped tests.

425. Answer: C

Explanation: Pytest is a Python testing framework that makes it easy to write and execute unit tests for Python programs.

426. Answer: B

Explanation: Selenium is a widely used open-source browser automation tool that can be used as part of testing, allowing tests to function as if a user were interacting with a browser.

427. Answer: B

Explanation: Lift and shift migration projects involve moving infrastructure and data from an on-premises data center to the cloud with minimal changes.

428. Answer: B

Explanation: When implementing a lift-and-shift migration, an inventory of all applications, data sources, and infrastructure should be performed to identify dependencies and influence the migration order.

429. Answer: C

Explanation: Katalon Studio is an open-source, interactive testing platform that builds on Selenium and can be used to test web-based mobile applications and APIs.

430. Answer: C

Explanation: Test-driven development (TDD) encourages developing small amounts of code and frequent testing, as tests are mapped to specific requirements and narrowly scoped.

431. Answer: C

Explanation: The Google Transfer Service is the recommended way of transferring data from AWS or other cloud providers to Google Cloud.

432. Answer: B

Explanation: The `gsutil` command-line utility is indeed recommended for transferring data from on-premises environments to Google Cloud Storage. It provides a robust set of commands and options for uploading, downloading, and managing objects in Google Cloud Storage buckets. `gsutil` supports parallel uploads and downloads, resumable transfers, and verification of data integrity during transfer, making it a versatile and efficient tool for handling large-scale data migrations and backups between on-premises systems and Google Cloud Storage.

433. Answer: C

Explanation: `gsutil` supports restarts after failures, which enhances data integrity and reliability during the transfer process. This capability allows `gsutil` to resume interrupted uploads or downloads from where they left off rather than starting over from the beginning. It ensures that large data transfers are not lost due to network issues, interruptions, or other failures, thereby maintaining the integrity and completeness of the data being transferred to or from Google Cloud Storage.

434. Answer: C

Explanation: The time required to transfer data is influenced by the volume of data, network bandwidth, and location of data, but not by the time of day.

435. Answer: C

Explanation: The largest Google Transfer Appliance has a capacity of 480 TB. This appliance is designed to facilitate large-scale data transfers by physically shipping the device to customers for uploading their data securely and efficiently into Google Cloud Storage.

436. Answer: D

Explanation: The `kubectl` component is a command-line tool used for managing Kubernetes clusters. It allows users to interact with Kubernetes clusters to deploy applications, inspect and manage cluster resources, and perform various administrative tasks. `kubectl` is essential for deploying and managing containerized applications within Kubernetes environments, providing commands to create, scale, update, and troubleshoot applications running on Kubernetes clusters.

437. Answer: D

Explanation: The cbt component is not installed by default and must be installed separately using the gcloud components install command

438. Answer: A

Explanation: User account authorization in Google Cloud Platform is managed through IAM roles and permissions. These roles define the access level a user or service account has over Google Cloud resources. To grant authorization, administrators assign appropriate IAM roles using the Google Cloud Console, `gcloud` command-line tool (`gcloud iam` commands), or programmatically through APIs. The `gcloud init` command, on the other hand, initializes the `gcloud` tool's configuration and prompts users to log in for authentication, but it does not directly manage authorization permissions.

439. Answer: B

Explanation: Time constraints on data transfer are one of the important factors to consider when transferring large volumes of data to Google Cloud.

440. Answer: B

Explanation: The `bq` command-line tool is specifically designed for working with Google BigQuery. It provides a convenient interface to interact with BigQuery datasets, tables, and queries directly from the command line. With `bq`, users can perform tasks such as creating and deleting datasets, loading data into BigQuery tables, running queries, exporting query results, managing table schemas, and more. It's an essential tool for developers, data engineers, and analysts who need to manage and query large datasets stored in Google BigQuery.

441. Answer: B

Explanation: When transferring data from an on-premises data center, using `gsutil` is a good option when the data volume is less than 10 TB and the network bandwidth is at least 100 Mbps.

442. Answer: B

Explanation: If no downtime is acceptable, you need to have two systems running in parallel: one in the cloud and one on-premises before switching over.

443. Answer: B

Explanation: Before migrating data, you should understand any regulations that cover that data, such as HIPAA in the United States or GDPR in the European Union, as well as any business-specific data governance policies.

444. Answer: B

Explanation: Cloud Operations Logging would be a good option if you are open to some modifications to the system for monitoring performance after migration.

445. Answer: A

Explanation: If a database SLA or other requirements do not allow for an export-based migration, you should consider creating a replica of the database in the Google Cloud, referred to as primary/replica or leader/follower configuration.

446. Answer: C

Explanation: Although important, the context does not specifically mention data encryption as a critical factor in planning data migration.

447. Answer: A

Explanation: You could modify the deployment process to use GCP services such as Cloud Build for automating deployment in the cloud.

448. Answer: B

Explanation: When the volume of data exceeds 20 TB, Google Transfer Appliance is often recommended for efficient data transfer to Google Cloud. This physical device allows large-scale data migration by securely shipping it to Google's data centers for upload to Google Cloud Storage. It provides a faster and more reliable method compared to transferring large datasets over the internet, especially in scenarios where bandwidth constraints or data privacy concerns are considerations.

449. Answer: B

Explanation: Locking the database for writes during an export operation can ensure a consistent export, especially for databases that are actively being modified. This practice helps prevent changes to the database state during the export process, ensuring that the exported data reflects a consistent snapshot at the time of export. By temporarily suspending write operations, databases can avoid exporting incomplete or inconsistent data, which is crucial for maintaining data integrity and reliability in backup and migration scenarios.

450. Answer: A

Explanation: If the volume of data is between 10 TB and 20 TB and network bandwidth is limited, use the Google Transfer Appliance if the time and cost requirements for gsutil are not acceptable.

VERSAtile Reads

About Our Products

Other products from VERSAtile Reads are:

 Elevate Your Leadership: The 10 Must-Have Skills

 Elevate Your Leadership: 8 Effective Communication Skills

 Elevate Your Leadership: 10 Leadership Styles for Every Situation

 300+ PMP Practice Questions Aligned with PMBOK 7, Agile Methods, and Key Process Groups – 2024

 Exam-Cram Essentials Last-Minute Guide to Ace the PMP Exam - Your Express Guide featuring PMBOK® Guide

 Career Mastery Blueprint - Strategies for Success in Work and Business

 Memory Magic: Unraveling the Secret of Mind Mastery

 The Success Equation Psychological Foundations For Accomplishment

 Fairy Dust Chronicles – The Short and Sweet of Wonder

 B2B Breakthrough – Proven Strategies from Real-World Case Studies

VERSAtile Reads

 CCSP Fast Track Master: CCSP Essentials for Exam Success

 CLF-C02: AWS Certified Cloud Practitioner: Fast Track to Exam Success

 ITIL 4 Foundation Essentials: Fast Track to Exam Success

 CCNP Security Essentials: Fast Track to Exam Success

 Certified SCRUM Master Exam Cram Essentials

 CISSP Fast Track: Master CISSP Essentials for Exam Success

 CISA Fast Track: Master CISA Essentials for Exam Success

 CISM Fast Track: Master CISM Essentials for Exam Success

 CCSP Fast Track: Master CCSP Essentials for Exam Success

 Certified SCRUM Master Exam Cram Essentials